The Praise of Folly

Desiderius

ERASMUS
THE PRAISE
OF FOLLY

Translated by John Wilson
1668

Ann Arbor Paperbacks

THE UNIVERSITY OF MICHIGAN PRESS

First edition as an Ann Arbor Paperback 1958

Manufactured in the United States of America

ERASMUS OF ROTTERDAM
to his friend
THOMAS MORE, health:

As I was coming awhile since out of Italy for England, that I might not waste all that time I was to sit on horseback in foolish and illiterate fables, I chose rather one while to revolve with myself something of our common studies, and other while to enjoy the remembrance of my friends, of whom I left here some no less learned than pleasant. Among these you, my More, came first in my mind, whose memory, though absent yourself, gives me such delight in my absence, as when present with you I ever found in your company; than which, let me perish if in all my life I ever met with anything more delectable. And therefore, being satisfied that something was to be done, and that that time was no wise proper for any serious matter, I resolved to make some sport with the praise of folly. But who the devil put that in your head? you'll say. The first thing was your surname of More, which comes

so near the word *Moriae* (folly) as you are far from
the thing. And that you are so, all the world will
clear you. In the next place, I conceived this exercise of wit would not be least approved by you;
inasmuch as you are wont to be delighted with
such kind of mirth, that is to say, neither unlearned,
if I am not mistaken, nor altogether insipid, and in
the whole course of your life have played the part
of a Democritus. And though such is the excellence
of your judgment that it was ever contrary to that
of the people's, yet such is your incredible affability
and sweetness of temper that you both can and delight to carry yourself to all men a man of all hours.
Wherefore you will not only with good will accept
this small declamation, but take upon you the defense of it, for as much as being dedicated to you,
it is now no longer mine but yours. But perhaps
there will not be wanting some wranglers that may
cavil and charge me, partly that these toys are
lighter than may become a divine, and partly more
biting than may beseem the modesty of a Christian,
and consequently exclaim that I resemble the ancient comedy, or another Lucian, and snarl at everything. But I would have them whom the lightness
or foolery of the argument may offend to consider
that mine is not the first of this kind, but the same
thing that has been often practiced even by great

authors: when Homer, so many ages since, did the like with the battle of frogs and mice; Virgil, with the gnat and puddings; Ovid, with the nut; when Polycrates and his corrector Isocrates extolled tyranny; Glauco, injustice; Favorinus, deformity and the quartan ague; Synescius, baldness; Lucian, the fly and flattery; when Seneca made such sport with Claudius' canonizations; Plutarch, with his dialogue between Ulysses and Gryllus; Lucian and Apuleius, with the ass; and some other, I know not who, with the hog that made his last will and testament, of which also even St. Jerome makes mention. And therefore if they please, let them suppose I played at tables for my diversion, or if they had rather have it so, that I rode on a hobbyhorse. For what injustice is it that when we allow every course of life its recreation, that study only should have none? Especially when such toys are not without their serious matter, and foolery is so handled that the reader that is not altogether thick-skulled may reap more benefit from it than from some men's crabbish and specious arguments. As when one, with long study and great pains, patches many pieces together on the praise of rhetoric or philosophy; another makes a panegyric to a prince; another encourages him to a war against the Turks; another tells you what will become of the world after himself is dead; and another finds out some new device for the better ordering of goat's wool: for as nothing is more trifling than to treat of serious matters triflingly, so nothing carries a better grace than so to discourse of trifles as a man may seem to have intended them least. For my own part, let other men judge of what I have written; though yet, unless an overweening opinion of myself may have made me blind in my own cause, I have praised folly, but not altogether foolishly. And now to say somewhat to that other cavil, of biting. This liberty was ever permitted to all men's wits, to make their smart, witty reflections on the common errors of mankind, and that too without offense, as long as this liberty does not run into licentiousness; which makes me the more admire the tender ears of the men of this age, that can away with solemn titles. No, you'll meet with some so preposterously religious that they will sooner endure the broadest scoffs even against Christ himself than hear the Pope or a prince be touched in the least, especially if it be anything that concerns their profit; whereas he that so taxes the lives of men, without naming anyone in particular, whither, I pray, may he be said to bite, or rather to teach and admonish? Or otherwise, I beseech you, under how many notions do I tax myself? Besides, he that spares no sort of men cannot be said to be angry with anyone in particular, but the vices of all. And therefore, if there shall happen to be anyone that shall say he is hit, he will but discover either his guilt or fear. Saint Jerome sported in this kind with more freedom and greater sharpness, not sparing sometimes men's very name. But I, besides that I have wholly avoided it, I have so moderated my style that the understanding reader will easily perceive my endeavors herein were rather to make mirth than bite. Nor have I, after the example of Juvenal, raked up that forgotten sink of filth and ribaldry, but laid before you things rather ridiculous than dishonest. And now, if there be anyone that is yet dissatisfied, let him at least remember that it is no dishonor to be discommended by Folly; and having brought her in speaking, it was but fit that I kept up the character of the person. But why do I run over these things to you, a person so excellent an advocate that no man better defends his client, though the cause many times be none of the best? Farewell, my best disputant More, and stoutly defend your *Moriae*.

From the country,
the 5th of the Ides of June.

THE PRAISE OF FOLLY

An oration, of feigned matter, spoken by Folly in her own person

At what rate soever the world talks of me (for I am not ignorant what an ill report Folly has got, even among the most foolish), yet that I am that she, that only she, whose deity recreates both gods and men, even this is a sufficient argument, that I no sooner stepped up to speak to this full assembly than all your faces put on a kind of new and unwonted pleasantness. So suddenly have you cleared your brows, and with so frolic and hearty a laughter given me your applause, that in truth as many of you as I behold on every side of me seem to me no less than Homer's gods drunk with nectar and nepenthe; whereas before, you sat as lumpish and pensive as if you had come from consulting an oracle. And as it usually happens when the sun begins to show his beams, or when after a sharp winter the spring breathes afresh on the earth, all things immediately get a new face, new color, and recover

as it were a certain kind of youth again: in like
manner, by but beholding me you have in an instant
gotten another kind of countenance; and so what the
otherwise great rhetoricians with their tedious and
long-studied orations can hardly effect, to wit, to remove the trouble of the mind, I have done it at once
with my single look.

But if you ask me why I appear before you in this
strange dress, be pleased to lend me your ears, and
I'll tell you; not those ears, I mean, you carry to
church, but abroad with you, such as you are wont
to prick up to jugglers, fools, and buffoons, and such
as our friend Midas once gave to Pan. For I am disposed awhile to play the sophist with you; not of
their sort who nowadays boozle young men's heads
with certain empty notions and curious trifles, yet
teach them nothing but a more than womanish
obstinacy of scolding: but I'll imitate those ancients
who, that they might the better avoid that infamous
appellation of *sophi* or *wise,* chose rather to be called
sophists. Their business was to celebrate the praises
of the gods and valiant men. And the like enco-
mium shall you hear from me, but neither of Hercules nor Solon, but my own dear self, that is to
say, Folly. Nor do I esteem a rush that call it a foolish
and insolent thing to praise one's self. Be it as foolish as they would make it, so they confess it proper:

and what can be more than that Folly be her own trumpet? For who can set me out better than myself, unless perhaps I could be better known to another than to myself? Though yet I think it somewhat more modest than the general practice of our nobles and wise men who, throwing away all shame, hire some flattering orator or lying poet from whose mouth they may hear their praises, that is to say, mere lies; and yet, composing themselves with a seeming modesty, spread out their peacock's plumes and erect their crests, while this impudent flatterer equals a man of nothing to the gods and proposes him as an absolute pattern of all virtue that's wholly a stranger to it, sets out a pitiful jay in other's feathers, washes the blackamoor white, and lastly swells a gnat to an elephant. In short, I will follow that old proverb that says, "He may lawfully praise himself that lives far from neighbors." Though, by the way, I cannot but wonder at the ingratitude, shall I say, or negligence of men who, notwithstanding they honor me in the first place and are willing enough to confess my bounty, yet not one of them for these so many ages has there been who in some thankful oration has set out the praises of Folly; when yet there has not wanted them whose elaborate endeavors have extolled tyrants, agues, flies, baldness, and such other pests of nature, to their own loss of both time and sleep. And now you shall hear from me a plain extemporary speech, but so much the truer. Nor would I have you think it like the rest of orators, made for the ostentation of wit; for these, as you know, when they have been beating their heads some thirty years about an oration and at last perhaps produce somewhat that was never their own, shall yet swear they composed it in three days, and that too for diversion: whereas I ever liked it best to speak whatever came first out.

But let none of you expect from me that after the manner of rhetoricians I should go about to define what I am, much less use any division; for I hold it equally unlucky to circumscribe her whose deity is universal, or make the least division in that worship about which everything is so generally agreed. Or to what purpose, think you, should I describe myself when I am here present before you, and you behold me speaking? For I am, as you see, that true and only giver of wealth whom the Greeks call *Moria*, the Latins *Stultitia*, and our plain English *Folly*. Or what need was there to have said so much, as if my very looks were not sufficient to inform you who I am? Or as if any man, mistaking me for wisdom, could not at first sight convince himself by my face the true index of my mind? I am no counterfeit, nor do I carry one thing in my looks and an-

other in my breast. No, I am in every respect so
like myself that neither can they dissemble me who
arrogate to themselves the appearance and title of
wise men and walk like asses in scarlet hoods, though
after all their hypocrisy Midas' ears will discover
their master. A most ungrateful generation of men
that, when they are wholly given up to my party,
are yet publicly ashamed of the name, as taking it
for a reproach; for which cause, since in truth they
are *morotatoi,* fools, and yet would appear to the
world to be wise men and Thales, we'll even call
them *morosophous,* wise fools.

Nor will it be amiss also to imitate the rhetoricians of our times, who think themselves in a manner gods if like horse leeches they can but appear
to be double-tongued, and believe they have done
a mighty act if in their Latin orations they can but
shuffle in some ends of Greek like mosaic work,
though altogether by head and shoulders and less
to the purpose. And if they want hard words, they
run over some worm-eaten manuscript and pick out
half a dozen of the most old and obsolete to confound their reader, believing, no doubt, that they
that understand their meaning will like it the better,
and they that do not will admire it the more by how
much the less they understand it. Nor is this way
of ours of admiring what seems most foreign with-

out its particular grace; for if there happen to be any more ambitious than others, they may give their applause with a smile, and, like the ass, shake their ears, that they may be thought to understand more than the rest of their neighbors.

But to come to the purpose: I have given you my name, but what epithet shall I add? What but that of the most foolish? For by what more proper name can so great a goddess as Folly be known to her disciples? And because it is not alike known to all from what stock I am sprung, with the Muses' good leave I'll do my endeavor to satisfy you. But yet neither the first Chaos, Orcus, Saturn, or Japhet, nor any of those threadbare, musty gods were my father, but Plutus, Riches; that only he, that is, in spite of Hesiod, Homer, nay and Jupiter himself, *divum pater atque hominum rex,* the father of gods and men, at whose single beck, as heretofore, so at present, all things sacred and profane are turned topsy-turvy. According to whose pleasure war, peace, empire, counsels, judgments, assemblies, wedlocks, bargains, leagues, laws, arts, all things light or serious—I want breath—in short, all the public and private business of mankind is governed; without whose help all that herd of gods of the poets' making, and those few of the better sort of the rest, either would not be at all, or if they were, they would be but such as live at home and keep a poor house to themselves. And to whomsoever he's an enemy, 'tis not Pallas herself that can befriend him; as on the contrary he whom he favors may lead Jupiter and his thunder in a string. This is my father and in him I glory. Nor did he produce me from his brain, as Jupiter that sour and ill-looked Pallas; but of that lovely nymph called Youth, the most beautiful and galliard of all the rest. Nor was I, like that limping blacksmith, begot in the sad and irksome bonds of matrimony. Yet, mistake me not, 'twas not that blind and decrepit Plutus in Aristophanes that got me, but such as he was in his full strength and pride of youth; and not that only, but at such a time when he had been well heated with nectar, of which he had, at one of the banquets of the gods, taken a dose extraordinary.

And as to the place of my birth, forasmuch as nowadays that is looked upon as a main point of nobility, it was neither, like Apollo's, in the floating Delos, nor Venus-like on the rolling sea, nor in any of blind Homer's as blind caves: but in the Fortunate Islands, where all things grew without plowing or sowing; where neither labor, nor old age, nor disease was ever heard of; and in whose fields neither daffodil, mallows, onions, beans, and such contemptible things would ever grow, but, on

the contrary, rue, angelica, bugloss, marjoram, tre-
foils, roses, violets, lilies, and all the gardens of
Adonis invite both your sight and your smelling.
And being thus born, I did not begin the world,
as other children are wont, with crying; but straight
perched up and smiled on my mother. Nor do I
envy to the great Jupiter the goat, his nurse, forasmuch as I was suckled by two jolly nymphs, to wit,
Drunkenness, the daughter of Bacchus, and Ignorance, of Pan. And as for such my companions and
followers as you perceive about me, if you have a
mind to know who they are, you are not like to be
the wiser for me, unless it be in Greek: this here,
which you observe with that proud cast of her eye,
is *Philantia,* Self-love; she with the smiling countenance, that is ever and anon clapping her hands,
is *Kolakia,* Flattery; she that looks as if she were
half asleep is *Lethe,* Oblivion; she that sits leaning
on both elbows with her hands clutched together is
Misoponia, Laziness; she with the garland on her
head, and that smells so strong of perfumes, is
Hedone, Pleasure; she with those staring eyes,
moving here and there, is *Anoia,* Madness; she with
the smooth skin and full pampered body is *Tryphe,*
Wantonness; and, as to the two gods that you see
with them, the one is *Komos,* Intemperance, the
other *Eegretos hypnos,* Dead Sleep. These, I say,

are my household servants, and by their faithful counsels I have subjected all things to my dominion and erected an empire over emperors themselves. Thus have you had my lineage, education, and companions.

And now, lest I may seem to have taken upon me the name of goddess without cause, you shall in the next place understand how far my deity extends, and what advantage by it I have brought both to gods and men. For, if it was not unwisely said by somebody, that this only is to be a god, to help men; and if they are deservedly enrolled among the gods that first brought in corn and wine and such other things as are for the common good of mankind, why am not I of right the *alpha,* or first, of all the gods? who being but one, yet bestow all things on all men. For first, what is more sweet or more precious than life? And yet from whom can it more properly be said to come than from me? For neither the crab-favoured Pallas' spear nor the cloud-gathering Jupiter's shield either beget or propagate mankind; but even he himself, the father of gods and king of men at whose very beck the heavens shake, must lay by his forked thunder and those looks wherewith he conquered the giants and with which at pleasure he frightens the rest of the gods, and like a common stage player put on a disguise as often as he goes about that, which now and then he does, that is to say the getting of children: And the Stoics too, that conceive themselves next to the gods, yet show me one of them, nay the veriest bigot of the sect, and if he do not put off his beard, the badge of wisdom, though yet it be no more than what is common with him and goats; yet at least he must lay by his supercilious gravity, smooth his forehead, shake off his rigid principles, and for some time commit an act of folly and dotage. In fine, that wise man whoever he be, if he intends to have children, must have recourse to me. But tell me, I beseech you, what man is that would submit his neck to the noose of wedlock, if, as wise men should, he did but first truly weigh the inconvenience of the thing? Or what woman is there would ever go to it did she seriously consider either the peril of child-bearing or the trouble of bringing them up? So then, if you owe your beings to wedlock, you owe that wedlock to this my follower, Madness; and what you owe to me I have already told you. Again, she that has but once tried what it is, would she, do you think, make a second venture if it were not for my other companion, Oblivion? Nay, even Venus herself, notwithstanding whatever Lucretius has said, would not deny but that all her virtue were lame and fruitless without the help of my deity. For out of that little, odd, ridiculous May-game came the supercilious philosophers, in whose room have succeeded a kind of people the world calls monks, cardinals, priests, and the most holy popes. And lastly, all that rabble of the poets' gods, with which heaven is so thwacked and thronged, that though it be of so vast an extent, they are hardly able to crowd one by another.

But I think it is a small matter that you thus owe your beginning of life to me, unless I also show you that whatever benefit you receive in the progress of it is of my gift likewise. For what other is this? Can that be called life where you take away pleasure? Oh! Do you like what I say? I knew none of you could have so little wit, or so much folly, or wisdom rather, as to be of any other opinion. For even the Stoics themselves that so severely cried down pleasure did but handsomely dissemble, and railed against it to the common people to no other end but that having discouraged them from it, they might the more plentifully enjoy it themselves. But tell me, by Jupiter, what part of man's life is that that is not sad, crabbed, unpleasant, insipid, troublesome, unless it be seasoned with pleasure, that is to say, folly? For the proof of which the never sufficiently praised Sophocles in that his happy elegy of us, "To know nothing is the only happiness," might be authority enough, but that I intend to take every particular by itself.

And first, who knows not but a man's infancy is the merriest part of life to himself, and most acceptable to others? For what is that in them which we kiss, embrace, cherish, nay enemies succor, but this witchcraft of folly, which wise Nature did of purpose give them into the world with them that they might the more pleasantly pass over the toil of education, and as it were flatter the care and diligence of their nurses? And then for youth, which is in such reputation everywhere, how do all men favor it, study to advance it, and lend it their helping hand? And whence, I pray, all this grace? Whence but from me? by whose kindness, as it understands as little as may be, it is also for that reason the higher privileged from exceptions; and I am mistaken if, when it is grown up and by experience and discipline brought to savor something like man, if in the same instant that beauty does not fade, its liveliness decay, its pleasantness grow flat, and its briskness fail. And by how much the further it runs from me, by so much the less it lives, till it comes to the burden of old age, not only hateful to others, but to itself also. Which also were altogether insupportable did not I pity its condition, in being present with it, and, as the poets' gods were wont to assist such as were dying with some pleasant metamorphosis, help their decrepitness as much as in me lies by bringing them back to a second childhood, from whence they are not improperly called twice children. Which, if you ask me how I do it, I shall not be shy in the point. I bring them to our River Lethe (for its springhead rises in the Fortunate Islands, and that other of hell is but a brook in comparison), from which, as soon as they have drunk down a long forgetfulness, they wash away by degrees the perplexity of their minds, and so wax young again.

But perhaps you'll say they are foolish and doting. Admit it; 'tis the very essence of childhood; as if to be such were not to be a fool, or that that condition had anything pleasant in it, but that it understood nothing. For who would not look upon that child as a prodigy that should have as much wisdom as a man?—according to that common proverb, "I do not like a child that is a man too soon." Or who would endure a converse or friendship with that old man who to so large an experience of things had joined an equal strength of mind and sharpness of judgment? And therefore for this reason it is that old age dotes; and that it does so, it is beholding to me. Yet, notwithstanding, is this dotard exempt from all those cares that distract a wise man; he is not the less pot companion, nor is he sensible of that burden of life which the more manly age finds enough to do to stand upright under it. And sometimes too, like Plautus' old man, he returns to his three letters, A.M.O., the most unhappy of all things living, if he rightly understood what he did in it. And yet, so much do I befriend him that I make him well received of his friends and no unpleasant companion; for as much as, according to Homer, Nestor's discourse was pleasanter than honey, whereas Achilles' was both bitter and malicious; and that of old men, as he has it in another place, florid. In which respect also they have this advantage of children, in that they want the only pleasure of the others' life, we'll suppose it prattling. Add to this that old men are more eagerly delighted with children, and they, again, with old men. "Like to like," quoted the Devil to the collier. For what difference between them, but that the one has more wrinkles and years upon his head than the other? Otherwise, the brightness of their hair, toothless mouth, weakness of body, love of mild, broken speech, chatting, toying, forgetfulness, inadvertency, and briefly, all other their actions agree in everything. And by how much the nearer they approach to this old age, by so much they grow backward into the likeness of children, until like them they pass from life to death, without any weariness of the one, or sense of the other.

And now, let him that will compare the benefits
they receive by me, the metamorphoses of the gods,
of whom I shall not mention what they have done
in their pettish humors but where they have been
most favorable: turning one into a tree, another into
a bird, a third into a grasshopper, serpent, or the
like. As if there were any difference between perish-
ing and being another thing! But I restore the same
man to the best and happiest part of his life. And
if men would but refrain from all commerce with
wisdom and give up themselves to be governed by
me, they should never know what it were to be old,
but solace themselves with a perpetual youth. Do
but observe our grim philosophers that are perpetually beating their brains on knotty subjects, and for
the most part you'll find them grown old before they
are scarcely young. And whence is it, but that their
continual and restless thoughts insensibly prey upon
their spirits and dry up their radical moisture?
Whereas, on the contrary, my fat fools are as plump
and round as a Westphalian hog, and never sensible
of old age, unless perhaps, as sometimes it rarely
happens, they come to be infected with wisdom, so
hard a thing it is for a man to be happy in all things.
And to this purpose is that no small testimony of
the proverb, that says, "Folly is the only thing that
keeps youth at a stay and old age afar off;" as it is
verified in the Brabanders, of whom there goes this

common saying, "That age, which is wont to render other men wiser, makes them the greater fools." And yet there is scarce any nation of a more jocund converse, or that is less sensible of the misery of old age, than they are. And to these, as in situation, so for manner of living, come nearest my friends the Hollanders. And why should I not call them mine, since they are so diligent observers of me that they are commonly called by my name?—of which they are so far from being ashamed, they rather pride themselves in it. Let the foolish world then be packing and seek out Medeas, Circes, Venuses, Auroras, and I know not what other fountains of restoring youth. I am sure I am the only person that both can, and have, made it good. 'Tis I alone that have that wonderful juice with which Memnon's daughter prolonged the youth of her grandfather Tithon. I am that Venus by whose favor Phaon became so young again that Sappho fell in love with him. Mine are those herbs, if yet there be any such, mine those charms, and mine that fountain that not only restores departed youth but, which is more desirable, preserves it perpetual. And if you all subscribe to this opinion, that nothing is better than youth or more execrable than age, I conceive you cannot but see how much you are indebted to me, that have retained so great a good and shut out so great an evil.

But why do I altogether spend my breath in speaking of mortals? View heaven round, and let him that will reproach me with my name if he find any one of the gods that were not stinking and contemptible were he not made acceptable by my deity. Why is it that Bacchus is always a stripling, and bushy-haired? but because he is mad, and drunk, and spends his life in drinking, dancing, revels, and May games, not having so much as the least society with Pallas. And lastly, he is so far from desiring to be accounted wise that he delights to be worshiped with sports and gambols; nor is he displeased with the proverb that gave him the surname of fool, "A greater fool than Bacchus;" which name of his was changed to Morychus, for that sitting before the gates of his temple, the wanton country people were wont to bedaub him with new wine and figs. And of scoffs, what not, have not the ancient comedies thrown on him? O foolish god, say they, and worthy to be born as you were of your father's thigh! And yet, who had not rather be your fool and sot, always merry, ever young, and making sport for other people, than either Homer's Jupiter with his crooked counsels, terrible to everyone; or old Pan with his hubbubs; or smutty Vulcan half covered with cinders; or even Pallas herself, so dreadful with her Gorgon's head and spear and a countenance like

bullbeef? Why is Cupid always portrayed like a
boy, but because he is a very wag and can neither do
nor so much as think of anything sober? Why Venus
ever in her prime, but because of her affinity with
me? Witness that color of her hair, so resembling
my father, from whence she is called the golden
Venus; and lastly, ever laughing, if you give any
credit to the poets, or their followers the statuaries.
What deity did the Romans ever more religiously
adore than that of Flora, the foundress of all pleasure? Nay, if you should but diligently search the
lives of the most sour and morose of the gods out
of Homer and the rest of the poets, you would find
them all but so many pieces of Folly. And to what
purpose should I run over any of the other gods'
tricks when you know enough of Jupiter's loose
loves? When that chaste Diana shall so far forget
her sex as to be ever hunting and ready to perish
for Endymion? But I had rather they should hear
these things from Momus, from whom heretofore
they were wont to have their shares, till in one of
their angry humors they tumbled him, together
with Ate, goddess of mischief, down headlong to
the earth, because his wisdom, forsooth, unseason-
ably disturbed their happiness. Nor since that dares
any mortal give him harbor, though I must confess
there wanted little but that he had been received
into the courts of princes, had not my companion

Flattery reigned in chief there, with whom and the other there is no more correspondence than between lambs and wolves. From whence it is that the gods play the fool with the greater liberty and more content to themselves "doing all things carelessly," as says Father Homer, that is to say, without anyone to correct them. For what ridiculous stuff is there which that stump of the fig tree Priapus does not afford them? What tricks and legerdemains with which Mercury does not cloak his thefts? What buffoonery that Vulcan is not guilty of, while one with his polt-foot, another with his smutched muzzle, another with his impertinencies, he makes sport for the rest of the gods? As also that old Silenus with his country dances, Polyphemus footing time to his Cyclops hammers, the nymphs with their jigs, and satyrs with their antics; while Pan makes them all twitter with some coarse ballad, which yet they had rather hear than the Muses themselves, and chiefly when they are well whittled with nectar. Besides, what should I mention what these gods do when they are half drunk? Now by my troth, so foolish that I myself can hardly refrain laughter. But in these matters 'twere better we remembered Harpocrates, lest some eavesdropping god or other take us whispering that which Momus only has the privilege of speaking at length.

And therefore, according to Homer's example,

I think it high time to leave the gods to themselves, and look down a little on the earth; wherein likewise you'll find nothing frolic or fortunate that it owes not to me. So provident has that great parent of mankind, Nature, been that there should not be anything without its mixture and, as it were, seasoning of Folly. For since according to the definition of the Stoics, wisdom is nothing else than to be governed by reason, and on the contrary Folly, to be given up to the will of our passions, that the life of man might not be altogether disconsolate and hard to away with, of how much more passion than reason has Jupiter composed us? putting in, as one would say, "scarce half an ounce to a pound." Besides, he has confined reason to a narrow corner of the brain and left all the rest of the body to our passions; has also set up, against this one, two as it were, masterless tyrants—anger, that possesses the region of the heart, and consequently the very fountain of life, the heart itself; and lust, that stretches its empire everywhere. Against which double force how powerful reason is let common experience declare, inasmuch as she, which yet is all she can do, may call out to us till she be hoarse again and tell us the rules of honesty and virtue; while they give up the reins to their governor and make a hideous clamor, till at last being wearied, he suffer himself to be carried whither they please to hurry him.

But forasmuch as such as are born to the business of the world have some little sprinklings of reason more than the rest, yet that they may the better manage it, even in this as well as in other things, they call me to counsel; and I give them such as is worthy of myself, to wit, that they take to them a wife—a silly thing, God wot, and foolish, yet wanton and pleasant, by which means the roughness of the masculine temper is seasoned and sweetened by her folly. For in that Plato seems to doubt under what genus he should put woman, to wit, that of rational creatures or brutes, he intended no other in it than to show the apparent folly of the sex. For if perhaps any of them goes about to be thought wiser than the rest, what else does she do but play the fool twice, as if a man should "teach a cow to dance," "a thing quite against the hair." For as it doubles the crime if anyone should put a disguise upon Nature, or endeavor to bring her to that she will in no wise bear, according to that proverb of the Greeks, "An ape is an ape, though clad in scarlet;" so a woman is a woman still, that is to say foolish, let her put on whatever vizard she please.

But, by the way, I hope that sex is not so foolish as to take offense at this, that I myself, being a woman, and Folly too, have attributed folly to them. For if they weigh it right, they needs must acknowl-edge that they owe it to folly that they are more fortunate than men. As first their beauty, which, and that not without cause, they prefer before everything, since by its means they exercise a tyranny even upon tyrants themselves; otherwise, whence proceeds that sour look, rough skin, bushy beard, and such other things as speak plain old age in a man, but from that disease of wisdom? Whereas women's cheeks are ever plump and smooth, their voice small, their skin soft, as if they imitated a certain kind of perpetual youth. Again, what greater thing do they wish in their whole lives than that they may please the man? For to what other purpose are all those dresses, washes, baths, slops, perfumes, and those several little tricks of setting their faces, painting their eyebrows, and smoothing their skins? And now tell me, what higher letters of recommendation have they to men than this folly? For what is it they do not permit them to do? And to what other purpose than that of pleasure? Wherein yet their folly is not the least thing that pleases; which so true it is, I think no one will deny, that does but consider with himself, what foolish discourse and odd gambols pass between a man and his woman, as often as he had a mind to be gamesome? And so I have shown you whence the first and chiefest delight of man's life springs.

But there are some, you'll say, and those too

none of the youngest, that have a greater kindness for the pot than the petticoat and place their chiefest pleasure in good fellowship. If there can be any great entertainment without a woman at it, let others look to it. This I am sure, there was never any pleasant which folly gave not the relish to. Insomuch that if they find no occasion of laughter, they send for "one that may make it," or hire some buffoon flatterer, whose ridiculous discourse may put by the gravity of the company. For to what purpose were it to clog our stomachs with dainties, junkets, and the like stuff, unless our eyes and ears, nay whole mind, were likewise entertained with jests, merriments, and laughter? But of these kind of second courses I am the only cook; though yet those ordinary practices of our feasts, as choosing a king, throwing dice, drinking healths, trolling it round, dancing the cushion, and the like, were not invented by the seven wise men but myself, and that too for the common pleasure of mankind. The nature of all which things is such that the more of folly they have, the more they conduce to human life, which, if it were unpleasant, did not deserve the name of life; and other than such it could not well be, did not these kind of diversions wipe away tediousness, next cousin to the other.

But perhaps there are some that neglect this way

of pleasure and rest satisfied in the enjoyment of their friends, calling friendship the most desirable of all things, more necessary than either air, fire, or water; so delectable that he that shall take it out of the world had as good put out the sun; and, lastly, so commendable, if yet that make anything to the matter, that neither the philosophers themselves doubted to reckon it among their chiefest good. But what if I show you that I am both the beginning and end of this so great good also? Nor shall I go about to prove it by fallacies, sorites, dilemmas, or other the like subtleties of logicians, but after my blunt way point out the thing as clearly as it were with my finger.

And now tell me if to wink, slip over, be blind at, or deceived in the vices of our friends, nay, to admire and esteem them for virtues, be not at least the next degree to folly? What is it when one kisses his mistress' freckle neck, another the wart on her nose? When a father shall swear his squint-eyed child is more lovely than Venus? What is this, I say, but mere folly? And so, perhaps you'll cry it is; and yet 'tis this only that joins friends together and continues them so joined. I speak of ordinary men, of whom none are born without their imperfections, and happy is he that is pressed with the least: for among wise princes there is either no friendship at all, or if there be, 'tis unpleasant and reserved, and that too but among a very few 'twere a crime to say none. For that the greatest part of mankind are fools, nay there is not anyone that dotes not in many things; and friendship, you know, is seldom made but among equals. And yet if it should so happen that there were a mutual good will between them, it is in no wise firm nor very long lived; that is to say, among such as are morose and more circumspect than needs, as being eagle-sighted into his friends' faults, but so blear-eyed to their own that they take not the least notice of the wallet that hangs behind their own shoulders. Since then the nature of man is such that there is scarce anyone to be found that is not subject to many errors, add to this the great diversity of minds and studies, so many slips, oversights, and chances of human life, and how is it possible there should be any true friendship between those Argus, so much as one hour, were it not for that which the Greeks excellently call *euetheian?* And you may render by folly or good nature, choose you whether. But what? Is not the author and parent of all our love, Cupid, as blind as a beetle? And as with him all colors agree, so from him is it that everyone likes his own sweeterkin best, though never so ugly, and "that an old man dotes on his old wife, and a boy on his girl."

These things are not only done everywhere but laughed at too; yet as ridiculous as they are, they make society pleasant, and, as it were, glue it together.

And what has been said of friendship may more reasonably be presumed of matrimony, which in truth is no other than an inseparable conjunction of life. Good God! What divorces, or what not worse than that, would daily happen were not the converse between a man and his wife supported and cherished by flattery, apishness, gentleness, ignorance, dissembling, certain retainers of mine also! Whoop holiday! how few marriages should we have, if the husband should but thoroughly examine how many tricks his pretty little mop of modesty has played before she was married! And how fewer of them would hold together, did not most of the wife's actions escape the husband's knowledge through his neglect or sottishness! And for this also you are beholden to me, by whose means it is that the husband is pleasant to his wife, the wife to her husband, and the house kept in quiet. A man is laughed at, when seeing his wife weeping he licks up her tears. But how much happier is it to be thus deceived than by being troubled with jealousy not only to torment himself but set all things in a hubbub!

In fine, I am so necessary to the making of all

society and manner of life both delightful and lasting, that neither would the people long endure their governors, nor the servant his master, nor the master his footman, nor the scholar his tutor, nor one friend another, nor the wife her husband, nor the usurer the borrower, nor a soldier his commander, nor one companion another, unless all of them had their interchangeable failings, one while flattering, other while prudently conniving, and generally sweetening one another with some small relish of folly.

And now you'd think I had said all, but you shall hear yet greater things. Will he, I pray, love anyone that hates himself? Or ever agree with another who is not at peace with himself? Or beget pleasure in another that is troublesome to himself? I think no one will say it that is not more foolish than Folly. And yet, if you should exclude me, there's no man but would be so far from enduring another that he would stink in his own nostrils, be nauseated with his own actions, and himself become odious to himself; forasmuch as Nature, in too many things rather a stepdame than a parent to us, has imprinted that evil in men, especially such as have least judgment, that everyone repents him of his own condition and admires that of others. Whence it comes to pass that all her gifts, elegancy, and graces corrupt and perish. For what benefit is beauty, the greatest blessing of heaven, if it be mixed with affectation? What youth, if corrupted with the severity of old age? Lastly, what is that in the whole business of a man's life he can do with any grace to himself or others —for it is not so much a thing of art, as the very life of every action, that it be done with a good mien —unless this my friend and companion, Self-love, be present with it? Nor does she without cause supply me the place of a sister, since her whole endeavors are to act my part everywhere. For what is more foolish than for a man to study nothing else than how to please himself? To make himself the object of his own admiration? And yet, what is there that is either delightful or taking, nay rather what not the contrary, that a man does against the hair? Take away this salt of life, and the orator may even sit still with his action, the musician with all his division will be able to please no man, the player be hissed off the stage, the poet and all his Muses ridiculous, the painter with his art contemptible, and the physician with all his slip-slops go a-begging. Lastly, you will be taken for an ugly fellow instead of youthful, and a beast instead of a wise man, a child instead of eloquent, and instead of a well-bred man, a clown. So necessary a thing it is that everyone flatter himself and commend himself to himself before he can be commended by others.

Lastly, since it is the chief point of happiness "that a man is willing to be what he is," you have further abridged in this my Self-love, that no man is ashamed of his own face, no man of his own wit, no man of his own parentage, no man of his own house, no man of his manner of living, nor any man of his own country; so that a Highlander has no desire to change with an Italian, a Thracian with an Athenian, nor a Scythian for the Fortunate Islands. O the singular care of Nature, that in so great a variety of things has made all equal! Where she has been sometimes sparing of her gifts she has recompensed it with the more of self-love; though here, I must confess, I speak foolishly, it being the greatest of all other her gifts: to say nothing that no great action was ever attempted without my motion, or art brought to perfection without my help.

Is not war the very root and matter of all famed enterprises? And yet what more foolish than to undertake it for I know what trifles, especially when both parties are sure to lose more than they get by the bargain? For of those that are slain, not a word of them; and for the rest, when both sides are close engaged "and the trumpets make an ugly noise," what use of those wise men, I pray, that are so exhausted with study that their thin, cold blood has scarce any spirits left? No, it must be those blunt, fat fellows, that by how much the more they exceed in courage, fall short in understanding. Unless perhaps one had rather choose Demosthenes for a soldier, who, following the example of Archilochius, threw away his arms and betook him to his heels e'er he had scarce seen his enemy; as ill a soldier, as happy an orator.

But counsel, you'll say, is not of least concern in matters of war. In a general I grant it; but this thing of warring is not part of philosophy, but managed by parasites, panders, thieves, cut-throats, plowmen, sots, spendthrifts, and such other dregs of mankind, not philosophers; who how unapt they are even for common converse, let Socrates, whom the oracle of Apollo, though not so wisely, judged "the wisest of all men living," be witness; who stepping up to speak somewhat, I know not what, in public was forced to come down again well laughed at for his pains. Though yet in this he was not altogether a fool, that he refused the appellation of wise, and returning it back to the oracle, delivered his opinion that a wise man should abstain from meddling with public business; unless perhaps he should have rather admonished us to beware of wisdom if we intended to be reckoned among the number of men, there being nothing but his wisdom that first accused and afterwards sentenced him to the drinking of his poisoned cup. For while, as you find him in Aristophanes, philosophizing about clouds and ideas, measuring how far a flea could leap, and admiring that so small a creature as a fly should make so great a buzz, he meddled not with anything that concerned common life. But his master being in danger of his head, his scholar Plato is at hand, to wit that famous patron, that being disturbed with the noise of the people, could not go through half his first sentence. What should I speak of Theophrastus, who being about to make an oration, became as dumb as if he had met a wolf in his way, which yet would have put courage in a man of war? Or Isocrates, that was so cowhearted that he dared never attempt it? Or Tully, that great founder of the Roman eloquence, that could never begin to speak without an odd kind of trembling, like a boy that had got the hiccough; which Fabius interprets as an argument of a wise orator and one that was sensible of what he was doing; and while he says it, does he not plainly confess that wisdom is a great obstacle to the true management of business? What would become of them, think you, were they to fight it out at blows that are so dead through fear when the contest is only with empty words?

And next to these is cried up, forsooth, that goodly sentence of Plato's, "Happy is that common-

wealth where a philosopher is prince, or whose
prince is addicted to philosophy." When yet if you
consult historians, you'll find no princes more pestilent to the commonwealth than where the empire
has fallen to some smatterer in philosophy or one
given to letters. To the truth of which I think the
Catoes give sufficient credit; of whom the one was
ever disturbing the peace of the commonwealth with
his hair-brained accusations; the other, while he too
wisely vindicated its liberty, quite overthrew it. Add
to this the Bruti, Casii, nay Cicero himself, that
was no less pernicious to the commonwealth of
Rome than was Demosthenes to that of Athens.
Besides M. Antoninus (that I may give you one
instance that there was once one good emperor; for
with much ado I can make it out) was become burdensome and hated of his subjects upon no other
score but that he was so great a philosopher. But
admitting him good, he did the commonwealth
more hurt in leaving behind him such a son as he
did than ever he did it good by his own government.
For these kind of men that are so given up to the
study of wisdom are generally most unfortunate,
but chiefly in their children; Nature, it seems, so
providently ordering it, lest this mischief of wisdom
should spread further among mankind. For which
reason it is manifest why Cicero's son was so degen-

erate, and that wise Socrates' children, as one has well observed, were more like their mother than their father, that is to say, fools.

However this were to be born with, if only as to public employments they were "like a sow upon a pair of organs," were they anything more apt to discharge even the common offices of life. Invite a wise man to a feast and he'll spoil the company, either with morose silence or troublesome disputes. Take him out to dance, and you'll swear "a cow would have done it better." Bring him to the theatre, and his very looks are enough to spoil all, till like Cato he take an occasion of withdrawing rather than put off his supercilious gravity. Let him fall into discourse, and he shall make more sudden stops than if he had a wolf before him. Let him buy, or sell, or in short go about any of those things without there is no living in this world, and you'll say this piece of wisdom were rather a stock than a man, of so little use is he to himself, country, or friends; and all because he is wholly ignorant of common things and lives a course of life quite different from the people; by which means it is impossible but that he contract a popular odium, to wit, by reason of the great diversity of their life and souls. For what is there at all done among men that is not full of folly, and that too from fools and to fools? Against which universal practice if any single one shall dare to set up his throat, my advice to him is, that following the example of Timon, he retire into some desert and there enjoy his wisdom to himself.

But, to return to my design, what power was it that drew those stony, oaken, and wild people into cities but flattery? For nothing else is signified by Amphion and Orpheus' harp. What was it that, when the common people of Rome were like to have destroyed all by their mutiny, reduced them to obedience? Was it a philosophical oration? Least. But a ridiculous and childish fable of the belly and the rest of the members. And as good success had Themistocles in his of the fox and hedgehog. What wise man's oration could ever have done so much with the people as Sertorius' invention of his white hind? Or his ridiculous emblem of pulling off a horse's tail hair by hair? Or as Lycurgus his example of his two whelps? To say nothing of Minos and Numa, both which ruled their foolish multitudes with fabulous inventions; with which kind of toys that great and powerful beast, the people, are led anyway. Again what city ever received Plato's or Aristotle's laws, or Socrates' precepts? But, on the contrary, what made the Decii devote themselves to the infernal gods, or Q. Curtius to leap into the gulf, but an empty vainglory, a most bewitching siren?

And yet 'tis strange it should be so condemned by those wise philosophers. For what is more foolish, say they, than for a suppliant suitor to flatter the people, to buy their favor with gifts, to court the applauses of so many fools, to please himself with their acclamations, to be carried on the people's shoulders as in triumph, and have a brazen statue in the marketplace? Add to this the adoption of names and surnames, those divine honors given to a man of no reputation, and the deification of the most wicked tyrants with public ceremonies; most foolish things, and such as one Democritus is too little to laugh at. Who denies it? And yet from this root sprang all the great acts of the heroes which the pens of so many eloquent men have extolled to the skies. In a word, this folly is that that laid the foundation of cities; and by it, empire, authority, religion, policy, and public actions are preserved; neither is there anything in human life that is not a kind of pastime of folly.

But to speak of arts, what set men's wits on work to invent and transmit to posterity so many famous, as they conceive, pieces of learning but the thirst of glory? With so much loss of sleep, such pains and travail, have the most foolish of men thought to purchase themselves a kind of I know not what fame, than which nothing can be more vain. And yet notwithstanding, you owe this advantage to folly, and which is the most delectable of all other, that you reap the benefit of other men's madness.

And now, having vindicated to myself the praise of fortitude and industry, what think you if I do the same by that of prudence? But some will say, you may as well join fire and water. It may be so. But yet I doubt not but to succeed even in this also, if, as you have done hitherto, you will but favor me with your attention. And first, if prudence depends upon experience, to whom is the honor of that name more proper? To the wise man, who partly out of modesty and partly distrust of himself, attempts nothing; or the fool, whom neither modesty which he never had, nor danger which he never considers, can discourage from anything? The wise man has recourse to the books of the ancients, and from thence picks nothing but subtleties of words. The fool, in undertaking and venturing on the business of the world, gathers, if I mistake not, the true prudence, such as Homer though blind may be said to have seen when he said, "The burnt child dreads the fire." For there are two main obstacles to the knowledge of things, modesty that casts a mist before the understanding, and fear that, having fancied a danger, dissuades us from the attempt. But from these folly sufficiently frees us, and few there are that rightly understand of what great advantage it is to blush at nothing and attempt everything.

But if you had rather take prudence for that that consists in the judgment of things, hear me, I beseech you, how far they are from it that yet crack of the name. For first 'tis evident that all human things, like Alcibiades' Sileni or rural gods, carry a double face, but not the least alike; so that what at first sight seems to be death, if you view it narrowly may prove to be life; and so the contrary. What appears beautiful may chance to be deformed; what wealthy, a very beggar; what infamous, praiseworthy; what learned, a dunce; what lusty, feeble; what jocund, sad; what noble, base; what lucky, unfortunate; what friendly, an enemy; and what healthful, noisome. In short, view the inside of these Sileni, and you'll find them quite other than what they appear; which, if perhaps it shall not seem so philosophically spoken, I'll make it plain to you "after my blunt way." Who would not conceive a prince a great lord and abundant in everything? But yet being so ill-furnished with the gifts of the mind, and ever thinking he shall never have enough, he's the poorest of all men. And then for his mind so given up to vice, 'tis a shame how it enslaves him. I might in like manner philosophize of the rest; but let this one, for example's sake, be enough.

Yet why this? will someone say. Have patience, and I'll show you what I drive at. If anyone seeing a player acting his part on a stage should go about to strip him of his disguise and show him to the people in his true native form, would he not, think you, not only spoil the whole design of the play, but deserve himself to be pelted off with stones as a phantastical fool and one out of his wits? But nothing is more common with them than such changes; the same person one while impersonating a woman, and another while a man; now a youngster, and by and by a grim seignior; now a king, and presently a peasant; now a god, and in a trice again an ordinary fellow. But to discover this were to spoil all, it being the only thing that entertains the eyes of the spectators. And what is all this life but a kind of comedy, wherein men walk up and down in one another's disguises and act their respective parts, till the property-man brings them back to the attiring house. And yet he often orders a different dress, and makes him that came but just now off in the robes of a king put on the rags of a beggar. Thus are all things represented by counterfeit, and yet without this there was no living.

And here if any wise man, as it were dropped from heaven, should start up and cry, this great thing whom the world looks upon for a god and I know not what is not so much as a man, for that like a beast he is led by his passions, but the worst of slaves, inasmuch as he gives himself up willingly to so many and such detestable masters. Again if he should bid a man that were bewailing the death of his father to laugh, for that he now began to live by having got an estate, without which life is but a kind of death; or call another that were boasting of his family ill begotten or base, because he is so far removed from virtue that is the only fountain of nobility; and so of the rest: what else would he get by it but be thought himself mad and frantic? For as nothing is more foolish than preposterous wisdom, so nothing is more unadvised than a forward unseasonable prudence. And such is his that does not comply with the present time "and order himself as the market goes," but forgetting that law of feasts, "either drink or begone," undertakes to disprove a common received opinion. Whereas on the contrary 'tis the part of a truly prudent man not to be wise beyond his condition, but either to take no notice of what the world does, or run with it for company. But this is foolish, you'll say; nor shall I deny it, provided always you be so civil on the other side as to confess that this is to act a part in that world.

But, O you gods, "shall I speak or hold my

tongue?" But why should I be silent in a thing that
is more true than truth itself? However it might not
be amiss perhaps in so great an affair to call forth
the Muses from Helicon, since the poets so often
invoke them upon every foolish occasion. Be present
then awhile, and assist me, you daughters of Jupiter,
while I make it out that there is no way to that so
much famed wisdom, nor access to that fortress as
they call it of happiness, but under the banner of
Folly. And first 'tis agreed of all hands that our passions belong to Folly; inasmuch as we judge a wise
man from a fool by this, that the one is ordered by
them, the other by reason; and therefore the Stoics
remove from a wise man all disturbances of mind as
so many diseases. But these passions do not only the
office of a tutor to such as are making towards the
port of wisdom, but are in every exercise of virtue
as it were spurs and incentives, nay and encouragers
to well doing: which though that great Stoic Seneca
most strongly denies, and takes from a wise man all
affections whatever, yet in doing that he leaves him
not so much as a man but rather a new kind of god
that was never yet nor ever like to be. Nay, to speak
plainer, he sets up a stony semblance of a man, void
of all sense and common feeling of humanity. And
much good to them with this wise man of theirs; let
them enjoy him to themselves, love him without

competitors, and live with him in Plato's commonwealth, the country of ideas, or Tantalus' orchards.
For who would not shun and startle at such a man,
as at some unnatural accident or spirit? A man dead
to all sense of nature and common affections, and no
more moved with love or pity than if he were a flint
or rock; whose censure nothing escapes; that com-
mits no errors himself, but has a lynx's eyes upon
others; measures everything by an exact line, and
forgives nothing; pleases himself with himself only;
the only rich, the only wise, the only free man, and
only king; in brief, the only man that is everything,
but in his own single judgment only; that cares not
for the friendship of any man, being himself a friend
to no man; makes no doubt to make the gods stoop
to him, and condemns and laughs at the whole actions of our life? And yet such a beast is this their
perfect wise man. But tell me pray, if the thing were
to be carried by most voices, what city would choose
him for its governor, or what army desire him for
their general? What woman would have such a
husband, what goodfellow such a guest, or what
servant would either wish or endure such a master?
Nay, who had not rather have one of the middle
sort of fools, who, being a fool himself, may the
better know how to command or obey fools; and
who though he please his like, 'tis yet the greater

number; one that is kind to his wife, merry among his friends, a boon companion, and easy to be lived with; and lastly one that thinks nothing of humanity should be a stranger to him? But I am weary of this wise man, and therefore I'll proceed to some other advantages.

Go to then. Suppose a man in some lofty high tower, and that he could look round him, as the poets say Jupiter was now and then wont. To how many misfortunes would he find the life of man subject? How miserable, to say no worse, our birth, how difficult our education; to how many wrongs our childhood exposed, to what pains our youth; how unsupportable our old age, and grievous our unavoidable death? As also what troops of diseases beset us, how many casualties hang over our heads, how many troubles invade us, and how little there is that is not steeped in gall? To say nothing of those evils one man brings upon another, as poverty, imprisonment, infamy, dishonesty, racks, snares, treachery, reproaches, actions, deceits—but I'm got into as endless a work as numbering the sands—for what offenses mankind have deserved these things, or what angry god compelled them to be born into such miseries is not my present business. Yet he that shall diligently examine it with himself, would he not, think you, approve the example of the Milesian virgins and kill himself? But who are they that for no other reason but that they were weary of life have hastened their own fate? Were they not the next neighbors to wisdom? among whom, to say nothing of Diogenes, Xenocrates, Cato, Cassius, Brutus, that wise man Chiron, being offered immortality, chose rather to die than be troubled with the same thing always.

And now I think you see what would become of the world if all men should be wise; to wit it were necessary we got another kind of clay and some better potter. But I, partly through ignorance, partly unadvisedness, and sometimes through forgetfulness of evil, do now and then so sprinkle pleasure with the hopes of good and sweeten men up in their greatest misfortunes that they are not willing to leave this life, even then when according to the account of the destinies this life has left them; and by how much the less reason they have to live, by so much the more they desire it; so far are they from being sensible of the least wearisomeness of life. Of my gift it is, that you have so many old Nestors everywhere that have scarce left them so much as the shape of a man; stutterers, dotards, toothless, gray-haired, bald; or rather, to use the words of Aristophanes, "Nasty, crumpled, miserable, shriveled, bald, toothless, and wanting their baubles," yet so delighted with life and to be thought young that one dyes his gray hairs; another covers his baldness with a periwig; another gets a set of new teeth; another falls desperately in love with a young wench and keeps more flickering about her than a young man would have been ashamed of. For to see such an old crooked piece with one foot in the grave to marry a plump young wench, and that too without a portion, is so common that men almost expect to be commended for it. But the best sport of all is to see our old women, even dead with age, and such skeletons one would think they had stolen out of their graves, and ever mumbling in their mouths, "Life is sweet;" and as old as they are, still caterwauling, daily plastering their face, scarce ever from the glass, gossiping, dancing, and writing love letters. These things are laughed at as foolish, as indeed they are; yet they please themselves, live merrily, swim in pleasure, and in a word are happy, by my courtesy. But I would have them to whom these things seem ridiculous to consider with themselves whether it be not better to live so pleasant a life in such kind of follies, than, as the proverb goes, "to take a halter and hang themselves." Besides though these things may be subject to censure, it concerns not my fools in the least, inasmuch as they take no notice of it; or if they do, they easily neglect it. If a stone fall upon a man's head, that's evil indeed; but dishonesty, infamy, villainy, ill reports carry no more hurt in them than a man is sensible of; and if a man have no sense of them, they are no longer evils. What are you the worse if the people hiss at you, so you applaud yourself? And that a man be able to do so, he must owe it to folly.

But methinks I hear the philosophers opposing it and saying 'tis a miserable thing for a man to be foolish, to err, mistake, and know nothing truly. Nay rather, this is to be a man. And why they should call it miserable, I see no reason; forasmuch as we are so born, so bred, so instructed, nay such is the common condition of us all. And nothing can be called miserable that suits with its kind, unless perhaps you'll think a man such because he can neither fly with birds, nor walk on all four with beasts, and is not armed with horns as a bull. For by the same reason he would call the warlike horse unfortunate, because he understood not grammar, nor ate cheese-cakes; and the bull miserable, because he'd make so ill a wrestler. And therefore, as a horse that has no skill in grammar is not miserable, no more is man in this respect, for that they agree with his nature. But again, the virtuosi may say that there was particularly added to man the knowledge of sciences, by whose help he might recompense him-

self in understanding for what nature cut him short
in other things. As if this had the least face of truth,
that Nature that was so solicitously watchful in the
production of gnats, herbs, and flowers should have
so slept when she made man, that he should have
need to be helped by sciences, which that old devil
Theuth, the evil genius of mankind, first invented
for his destruction, and are so little conducive to
happiness that they rather obstruct it; to which
purpose they are properly said to be first found out,
as that wise king in Plato argues touching the invention of letters.

Sciences therefore crept into the world with other
the pests of mankind, from the same head from
whence all other mischiefs spring; we'll suppose it
devils, for so the name imports when you call them
demons, that is to say, knowing. For that simple
people of the golden age, being wholly ignorant of
everything called learning, lived only by the guidance and dictates of nature; for what use of grammar, where every man spoke the same language and
had no further design than to understand one another? What use of logic, where there was no bicker-
ing about the double-meaning words? What need of
rhetoric, where there were no lawsuits? Or to what
purpose laws, where there were no ill manners? from
which without doubt good laws first came. Besides,

they were more religious than with an impious curiosity to dive into the secrets of nature, the dimension of stars, the motions, effects, and hidden causes of things; as believing it a crime for any man to attempt to be wise beyond his condition. And as to the inquiry of what was beyond heaven, that madness never came into their heads. But the purity of the golden age declining by degrees, first, as I said before, arts were invented by the evil genii; and yet but few, and those too received by fewer. After that the Chaldean superstition and Greek newfangledness, that had little to do, added I know not how many more; mere torments of wit, and that so great that even grammar alone is work enough for any man for his whole life.

Though yet among these sciences those only are in esteem that come nearest to common sense, that is to say, folly. Divines are half starved, naturalists out of heart, astrologers laughed at, and logicians slighted; only the physician is worth all the rest. And among them too, the more unlearned, impudent, or unadvised he is, the more he is esteemed, even among princes. For physic, especially as it is now professed by most men, is nothing but a branch of flattery, no less than rhetoric. Next them, the second place is given to our law-drivers, if not the first, whose profession, though I say it myself, most men laugh at as the ass of philosophy; yet there's scarce any business, either so great or so small, but is managed by these asses. These purchase their great lordships, while in the meantime the divine, having run through the whole body of divinity, sits gnawing a radish and is in continual warfare with lice and fleas. As therefore those arts are best that have the nearest affinity with folly, so are they most happy of all others that have least commerce with sciences and follow the guidance of Nature, who is in no wise imperfect, unless perhaps we endeavor to leap over those bounds she has appointed to us. Nature hates all false coloring and is ever best where she is least adulterated with art.

Go to then, don't you find among the several kinds of living creatures that they thrive best that understand no more than what Nature taught them? What is more prosperous or wonderful than the bee? And though they have not the same judgment of sense as other bodies have, yet wherein has architecture gone beyond their building of houses? What philosopher ever founded the like republic? Whereas the horse, that comes so near man in understanding and is therefore so familiar with him, is also partaker of his misery. For while he thinks it a shame to lose the race, it often happens that he cracks his wind; and in the battle, while he contends

for victory, he's cut down himself, and, together
with his rider "lies biting the earth;" not to mention
those strong bits, sharp spurs, close stables, arms,
blows, rider, and briefly, all that slavery he willingly
submits to, while, imitating those men of valor, he
so eagerly strives to be revenged of the enemy. Than
which how much more were the life of flies or birds
to be wished for, who living by the instinct of nature, look no further than the present, if yet man
would but let them alone in it. And if at anytime
they chance to be taken, and being shut up in cages
endeavor to imitate our speaking, 'tis strange how
they degenerate from their native gaiety. So much
better in every respect are the works of nature than
the adulteries of art.

In like manner I can never sufficiently praise that
Pythagoras in a dunghill cock, who being but one
had been yet everything, a philosopher, a man, a
woman, a king, a private man, a fish, a horse, a frog,
and, I believe too, a sponge; and at last concluded
that no creature was more miserable than man, for
that all other creatures are content with those bounds
that nature set them, only man endeavors to exceed
them. And again, among men he gives the preced-
ency not to the learned or the great, but the fool.
Nor had that Gryllus less wit than Ulysses with his
many counsels, who chose rather to lie grunting in

a hog sty than be exposed with the other to so many hazards. Nor does Homer, that father of trifles, dissent from me; who not only called all men "wretched and full of calamity," but often his great pattern of wisdom, Ulysses, "miserable;" Paris, Ajax, and Achilles nowhere. And why, I pray but that, like a cunning fellow and one that was his craft's master, he did nothing without the advice of Pallas? In a word he was too wise, and by that means ran wide of nature. As therefore among men they are least happy that study wisdom, as being in this twice fools, that when they are born men, they should yet so far forget their condition as to affect the life of gods; and after the example of the giants, with their philosophical gimcracks make a war upon nature: so they on the other side seem as little miserable as is possible who come nearest to beasts and never attempt anything beyond man. Go to then, let's try how demonstrable this is; not by enthymemes or the imperfect syllogisms of the Stoics, but by plain, downright, and ordinary examples.

And now, by the immortal gods! I think nothing more happy than that generation of men we commonly call fools, idiots, lack-wits, and dolts; splendid titles too, as I conceive them. I'll tell you a thing, which at first perhaps may seem foolish and absurd, yet nothing more true. And first they are not afraid of death—no small evil, by Jupiter! They are not tormented with the conscience of evil acts, not terrified with the fables of ghosts, nor frightened with spirits and goblins. They are not distracted with the fear of evils to come nor the hopes of future good. In short, they are not disturbed with those thousand of cares to which this life is subject. They are neither modest, nor fearful, nor ambitious, nor envious, nor love they any man. And lastly, if they should come nearer even to the very ignorance of brutes, they could not sin, for so hold the divines. And now tell me, you wise fool, with how many troublesome cares your mind is continually perplexed; heap together all the discommodities of your life, and then you'll be sensible from how many evils I have delivered my fools. Add to this that they are not only merry, play, sing, and laugh themselves, but make mirth wherever they come, a special privilege it seems the gods have given them to refresh the pensiveness of life. Whence it is that whereas the world is so differently affected one towards another, that all men indifferently admit them as their companions, desire, feed, cherish, embrace them, take their parts upon all occasions, and permit them without offense to do or say what they like. And so little does everything desire to hurt them, that even the very beasts, by a kind of natural instinct of their innocence no doubt, pass by their injuries. For of them it may be truly said that they are consecrate to the gods, and therefore and not without cause do men have them in such esteem. Whence is it else that they are in so great request with princes that they can neither eat nor drink, go anywhere, or be an hour without them? Nay, and in some degree they prefer these fools before their crabbish wise men, whom yet they keep about them for state's sake. Nor do I conceive the reason so difficult, or that it should seem strange why they are preferred before the others, for that these wise men speak to princes about nothing but grave, serious matters, and trusting to their own parts and learning do not fear sometimes "to grate their tender ears with smart truths;" but fools fit them with that they most delight in, as jests, laughter, abuses of other men, wanton pastimes, and the like.

Again, take notice of this no contemptible blessing which Nature has given fools, that they are the only plain, honest men and such as speak truth. And what is more commendable than truth? For though that proverb of Alcibiades in Plato attributes truth to drunkards and children, yet the praise of it is particularly mine, even from the testimony of Euripides, among whose other things there is extant that his honorable saying concerning us, "A fool speaks foolish things." For whatever a fool has in his heart, he both shows it in his looks and expresses it in his discourse; while the wise men's are those two tongues which the same Euripides mentions, whereof the one speaks truth, the other what they judge most seasonable for the occasion. These are they "that turn black into white," blow hot and cold with the same breath, and carry a far different meaning in their breast from what they feign with their tongue. Yet in the midst of all their prosperity, princes in this respect seem to me most unfortunate, because, having no one to tell them truth, they are forced to receive flatterers for friends.

But, someone may say, the ears of princes are strangers to truth, and for this reason they avoid those wise men, because they fear lest someone more frank than the rest should dare to speak to them things rather true than pleasant; for so the matter is, that they don't much care for truth. And yet this is found by experience among my fools, that not only truths but even open reproaches are heard with pleasure; so that the same thing which, if it came from a wise man's mouth might prove a capital crime, spoken by a fool is received with delight. For truth carries with it a certain peculiar power of pleasing, if no accident fall in to give occasion of offense; which faculty the gods have given only to fools. And for the same reasons is it that women are so earnestly delighted with this kind of men, as being more propense by nature to pleasure and toys. And whatsoever they may happen to do with them, although sometimes it be of the most serious, yet they turn it to jest and laughter, as that sex was ever quickwitted, especially to color their own faults.

But to return to the happiness of fools, who when they have passed over this life with a great deal of pleasantness and without so much as the least fear or sense of death, they go straight forth into the Elysian field, to recreate their pious and careless souls with such sports as they used here. Let's proceed then, and compare the condition of any of your wise men with that of this fool. Fancy to me now some example of wisdom you'd set up against him; one that had spent his childhood and youth in learning the sciences and lost the sweetest part of his life in watchings, cares, studies, and for the remaining part of it never so much as tasted the least of pleasure; ever sparing, poor, sad, sour, unjust, and rigorous to himself, and troublesome and hateful to others; broken with paleness, leanness, crassness, sore eyes, and an old age and death contracted before their time (though yet, what matter is it, when he die that never lived?); and such is the picture of this great wise man.

And here again do those frogs of the Stoics croak

at me and say that nothing is more miserable than
madness. But folly is the next degree, if not the very
thing. For what else is madness than for a man to
be out of his wits? But to let them see how they are
clean out of the way, with the Muses' good favor
we'll take this syllogism in pieces. Subtly argued, I
must confess, but as Socrates in Plato teaches us how
by splitting one Venus and one Cupid to make two
of either, in like manner should those logicians have
done and distinguished madness from madness, if
at least they would be thought to be well in their
wits themselves. For all madness is not miserable, or
Horace had never called his poetical fury a beloved
madness; nor Plato placed the raptures of poets,
prophets, and lovers among the chiefest blessings of
this life; nor that sibyl in Virgil called Aeneas'
travels mad labors. But there are two sorts of madness, the one that which the revengeful Furies send
privily from hell, as often as they let loose their
snakes and put into men's breasts either the desire of
war, or an insatiate thirst after gold, or some dishonest love, or parricide, or incest, or sacrilege, or the like
plagues, or when they terrify some guilty soul with
the conscience of his crimes; the other, but nothing
like this, that which comes from me and is of all
other things the most desirable; which happens as
often as some pleasing dotage not only clears the

mind of its troublesome cares but renders it more jocund. And this was that which, as a special blessing of the gods, Cicero, writing to his friend Atticus, wished to himself, that he might be the less sensible of those miseries that then hung over the commonwealth.

Nor was that Grecian in Horace much wide of it, who was so far made that he would sit by himself whole days in the theatre laughing and clapping his hands, as if he had seen some tragedy acting, whereas in truth there was nothing presented; yet in other things a man well enough, pleasant among his friends, kind to his wife, and so good a master to his servants that if they had broken the seal of his bottle, he would not have run mad for it. But at last, when by the care of his friends and physic he was freed from his distemper and become his own man again, he thus expostulates with them, "Now, by Pollux, my friends, you have rather killed than preserved me in thus forcing me from my pleasure." By which you see he liked it so well that he lost it against his will. And trust me, I think they were the madder of the two, and had the greater need of hellebore, that should offer to look upon so pleasant a madness as an evil to be removed by physic; though yet I have not determined whether every distemper of the sense or understanding be to be called madness.

For neither he that having weak eyes should take a mule for an ass, nor he that should admire an insipid poem as excellent would be presently thought mad; but he that not only errs in his senses but is deceived also in his judgment, and that too more than ordinary and upon all occasions—he, I must confess, would be thought to come very near to it. As if anyone hearing an ass bray should take it for excellent music, or a beggar conceive himself a king. And yet this kind of madness, if, as it commonly happens, it turn to pleasure, it brings a great delight not only to them that are possessed with it but to those also that behold it, though perhaps they may not be altogether so mad as the other, for the species of this madness is much larger than the people take it to be. For one mad man laughs at another, and beget themselves a mutual pleasure. Nor does it seldom happen that he that is the more mad, laughs at him that is less mad. And in this every man is the more happy in how many respects the more he is mad; and if I were judge in the case, he should be ranged in that class of folly that is peculiarly mine, which in truth is so large and universal that I scarce know anyone in all mankind that is wise at all hours, or has not some tang or other of madness.

And to this class do they appertain that slight everything in comparison of hunting and protest they take an unimaginable pleasure to hear the yell of the horns and the yelps of the hounds, and I believe could pick somewhat extraordinary out of their very excrement. And then what pleasure they take to see a buck or the like unlaced? Let ordinary fellows cut up an ox or a wether, 'twere a crime to have this done by anything less than a gentleman! who with his hat off, on his bare knees, and a couteau for that purpose (for every sword or knife is not allowable), with a curious superstition and certain postures, lays open the several parts in their respective order; while they that hem him in admire it with silence, as some new religious ceremony, though perhaps they have seen it a hundred times before. And if any of them chance to get the least piece of it, he presently thinks himself no small gentleman. In all which they drive at nothing more than to become beasts themselves, while yet they imagine they live the life of princes.

And next these may be reckoned those that have such an itch of building; one while changing rounds into squares, and presently again squares into rounds, never knowing either measure or end, till at last, reduced to the utmost poverty, there remains not to them so much as a place where they may lay their head, or wherewith to fill their bellies. And why all this? but that they may pass over a few years in feeding their foolish fancies.

And, in my opinion, next these may be reckoned such as with their new inventions and occult arts undertake to change the forms of things and hunt all about after a certain fifth essence; men so bewitched with this present hope that it never repents them of their pains or expense, but are ever contriving how they may cheat themselves, till, having spent all, there is not enough left them to provide another furnace. And yet they have not done dreaming these their pleasant dreams but encourage others, as much as in them lies, to the same happiness. And at last, when they are quite lost in all their expectations, they cheer up themselves with this sentence, "In great things the very attempt is enough," and then complain of the shortness of man's life that is not sufficient for so great an understanding.

And then for gamesters, I am a little doubtful whether they are to be admitted into our college; and yet 'tis a foolish and ridiculous sight to see some addicted so to it that they can no sooner hear the rattling of the dice but their heart leaps and dances again. And then when time after time they are so far drawn on with the hopes of winning that they have made shipwreck of all, and having split their ship on that rock of dice, no less terrible than the bishop and his clerks, scarce got alive to shore, they

choose rather to cheat any man of their just debts
than not pay the money they lost, lest otherwise, forsooth, they be thought no men of their words. Again
what is it, I pray, to see old fellows and half blind
to play with spectacles? Nay, and when a justly deserved gout has knotted their knuckles, to hire a
caster, or one that may put the dice in the box for
them? A pleasant thing, I must confess, did it not
for the most part end in quarrels, and therefore belongs rather to the Furies than me.

But there is no doubt but that that kind of men
are wholly ours who love to hear or tell feigned miracles and strange lies and are never weary of any tale,
though never so long, so it be of ghosts, spirits, goblins, devils, or the like; which the further they
are from truth, the more readily they are believed and the more do they tickle their itching
ears. And these serve not only to pass away time
but bring profit, especially to mass priests and par-
doners. And next to these are they that have gotten a foolish but pleasant persuasion that if they
can but see a wooden or painted Polypheme Christopher, they shall not die that day; or do but salute
a carved Barbara, in the usual set form, that he shall
return safe from battle; or make his application to
Erasmus on certain days with some small wax candles and proper prayers, that he shall quickly be

rich. Nay, they have gotten a Hercules, another Hippolytus, and a St. George, whose horse most religiously set out with trappings and bosses there wants little but they worship; however, they endeavor to make him their friend by some present or other, and to swear by his master's brazen helmet is an oath for a prince. Or what should I say of them that hug themselves with their counterfeit pardons; that have measured purgatory by an hourglass, and can without the least mistake demonstrate its ages, years, months, days, hours, minutes, and seconds, as it were in a mathematical table? Or what of those who, having confidence in certain magical charms and short prayers invented by some pious imposter, either for his soul's health or profit's sake, promise to themselves everything: wealth, honor, pleasure, plenty, good health, long life, lively old age, and the next place to Christ in the other world, which yet they desire may not happen too soon, that is to say before the pleasures of this life have left them?

And now suppose some merchant, soldier, or judge, out of so many rapines, parts with some small piece of money. He straight conceives all that sink of his whole life quite cleansed; so many perjuries, so many lusts, so many debaucheries, so many contentions, so many murders, so many deceits, so many breaches of trusts, so many treacheries bought off, as it were by compact; and so bought off that they may begin upon a new score. But what is more foolish than those, or rather more happy, who daily reciting those seven verses of the Psalms promise to themselves more than the top of felicity? Which magical verses some devil or other, a merry one without doubt but more a blab of his tongue than crafty, is believed to have discovered to St. Bernard, but not without a trick. And these are so foolish that I am half ashamed of them myself, and yet they are approved, and that not only by the common people but even the professors of religion. And what, are not they also almost the same where several countries avouch to themselves their peculiar saint, and as everyone of them has his particular gift, so also his particular form of worship? As, one is good for the toothache; another for groaning women; a third, for stolen goods; a fourth, for making a voyage prosperous; and a fifth, to cure sheep of the rot; and so of the rest, for it would be too tedious to run over all. And some there are that are good for more things than one; but chiefly, the Virgin Mother, to whom the common people do in a manner attribute more than to the Son.

Yet what do they beg of these saints but what belongs to folly? To examine it a little. Among all those offerings which are so frequently hung up in churches, nay up to the very roof of some of them, did you ever see the least acknowledgment from anyone that had left his folly, or grown a hair's breadth the wiser? One escapes a shipwreck, and he gets safe to shore. Another, run through in a duel, recovers. Another, while the rest were fighting, ran out of the field, no less luckily than valiantly. Another, condemned to be hanged, by the favor of some saint or other, a friend to thieves, got off himself by impeaching his fellows. Another escaped by breaking prison. Another recovered from his fever in spite of his physician. Another's poison turning to a looseness proved his remedy rather than death; and that to his wife's no small sorrow, in that she lost both her labor and her charge. Another's cart broke, and he saved his horses. Another preserved from the fall of a house. All these hang up their tablets, but no one gives thanks for his recovery from folly; so sweet a thing it is not to be wise, that on the contrary men rather pray against anything than folly.

But why do I launch out into this ocean of superstitions? Had I a hundred tongues, as many mouths, and a voice never so strong, yet were I not able to run over the several sorts of fools or all the names of folly, so thick do they swarm everywhere. And yet your priests make no scruple to receive and cherish them as proper instruments of profit; whereas if

some scurvy wise fellow should step up and speak
things as they are, as, to live well is the way to die
well; the best way to get quit of sin is to add to the
money you give the hatred of sin, tears, watchings,
prayers, fastings, and amendment of life; such or
such a saint will favor you, if you imitate his life—
these, I say, and the like—should this wise man chat
to the people, from what happiness into how great
troubles would he draw them?

Of this college also are they who in their lifetime
appoint with what solemnity they'll be buried, and
particularly set down how many torches, how many
mourners, how many singers, how many almsmen
they will have at it; as if any sense of it could come
to them, or that it were a shame to them that their
corpse were not honorably interred; so curious are
they herein, as if, like the aediles of old, these were to
present some shows or banquet to the people.

And though I am in haste, yet I cannot yet pass
by them who, though they differ nothing from the
meanest cobbler, yet 'tis scarcely credible how they
flatter themselves with the empty title of nobility.
One derives his pedigree from Aeneas, another from
Brutus, a third from the star by the tail of Ursa
Major. They show you on every side the statues and
pictures of their ancestors; run over their great-
grandfathers and the great-great-grandfathers of

both lines, and the ancient matches of their families, when themselves yet are but once removed from a statue, if not worse than those trifles they boast of. And yet by means of this pleasant self-love they live a happy life. Nor are they less fools who admire these beasts as if they were gods.

But what do I speak of any one or the other particular kind of men, as if this self-love had not the same effect everywhere and rendered most men superabundantly happy? As when a fellow, more deformed than a baboon, shall believe himself handsomer than Homer's Nereus. Another, as soon as he can draw two or three lines with a compass, presently thinks himself a Euclid. A third, that understands music no more than my horse, and for his voice as hoarse as a dunghill cock, shall yet conceive himself another Hermogenes. But of all madness that's the most pleasant when a man, seeing another any way excellent in what he pretends to himself, makes his boasts of it as confidently as if it were his own. And such was that rich fellow in Seneca, who whenever he told a story had his servants at his elbow to prompt him the names; and to that height had they flattered him that he did not question but he might venture a rubber at cuffs, a man otherwise so weak he could scarce stand, only presuming on this, that he had a company of sturdy servants about him.

Or to what purpose is it I should mind you of our professors of arts? Forasmuch as this self-love is so natural to them all that they had rather part with their father's land than their foolish opinions; but chiefly players, fiddlers, orators, and poets, of which the more ignorant each of them is, the more insolently he pleases himself, that is to say vaunts and spreads out his plumes. And like lips find like lettuce; nay, the more foolish anything is, the more 'tis admired, the greater number being ever tickled at the worst things, because, as I said before, most men are so subject to folly. And therefore if the more foolish a man is, the more he pleases himself and is admired by others, to what purpose should he beat his brains about true knowledge, which first will cost him dear, and next render him the more troublesome and less confident, and lastly, please only a few?

And now I consider it, Nature has planted, not only in particular men but even in every nation, and scarce any city is there without it, a kind of common self-love. And hence is it that the English, besides other things, particularly challenge to themselves beauty, music, and feasting. The Scots are proud of their nobility, alliance to the crown, and logical subtleties. The French think themselves the only well-bred men. The Parisians, excluding all others, arrogate to themselves the only knowledge of divinity.

The Italians affirm they are the only masters of good letters and eloquence, and flatter themselves on this account, that of all others they only are not barbarous. In which kind of happiness those of Rome claim the first place, still dreaming to themselves of somewhat, I know not what, of old Rome. The Venetians fancy themselves happy in the opinion of their nobility. The Greeks, as if they were the only authors of sciences, swell themselves with the titles of the ancient heroes. The Turk, and all that sink of the truly barbarous, challenge to themselves the only glory of religion and laugh at Christians as superstitious. And much more pleasantly the Jews expect to this day the coming of the Messiah, and so obstinately contend for their Law of Moses. The Spaniards give place to none in the reputation of soldiery. The Germans pride themselves in their tallness of stature and skill in magic.

And, not to instance in every particular, you see, I conceive, how much satisfaction this Self-love, who has a sister also not unlike herself called Flattery, begets everywhere; for self-love is no more than the soothing of a man's self, which, done to another, is flattery. And though perhaps at this day it may be thought infamous, yet it is so only with them that are more taken with words than things. They think truth is inconsistent with flattery, but that it is much otherwise we may learn from the examples of true beasts. What more fawning than a dog? And yet what more trusty? What has more of those little tricks than a squirrel? And yet what more loving to man? Unless, perhaps you'll say, men had better converse with fierce lions, merciless tigers, and furious leopards. For that flattery is the most pernicious of all things, by means of which some treacherous persons and mockers have run the credulous into such mischief. But this of mine proceeds from a certain gentleness and uprightness of mind and comes nearer to virtue than its opposite, austerity, or a morose and troublesome peevishness, as Horace calls it. This supports the dejected, relieves the distressed, encourages the fainting, awakens the stupid, refreshes the sick, supplies the untractable, joins loves together, and keeps them so joined. It entices children to take their learning, makes old men frolic, and, under the color of praise, does without offense both tell princes their faults and show them the way to amend them. In short, it makes every man the more jocund and acceptable to himself, which is the chiefest point of felicity. Again, what is more friendly than when two horses scrub one another? And to say nothing of it, that it's a main part of physic, and the only thing in poetry; 'tis the delight and relish of all human society.

But 'tis a sad thing, they say, to be mistaken. Nay rather, he is most miserable that is not so. For they are quite beside the mark that place the happiness of men in things themselves, since it only depends upon opinion. For so great is the obscurity and variety of human affairs that nothing can be clearly known, as it is truly said by our academics, the least insolent of all the philosophers; or if it could, it would but obstruct the pleasure of life. Lastly, the mind of man is so framed that it is rather taken with the false colors than truth; of which if anyone has a mind to make the experiment, let him go to church and hear sermons, in which if there be anything serious delivered, the audience is either asleep, yawning, or weary of it; but if the preacher—pardon my mistake, I would have said declaimer—as too often it happens, fall but into an old wives' story, they're presently awake, prick up their ears and gape after it. In like manner, if there be any poetical saint, or one of whom there goes more stories than ordinary, as for example, a George, a Christopher, or a Barbara, you shall see him more religiously worshiped than Peter, Paul, or even Christ himself. But these things are not for this place.

And now at how cheap a rate is this happiness purchased! Forasmuch as to the thing itself a man's whole endeavor is required, be it never so inconsiderable; but the opinion of it is easily taken up, which yet conduces as much or more to happiness. For suppose a man were eating rotten stockfish, the very smell of which would choke another, and yet believed it a dish for the gods, what difference is there as to his happiness? Whereas on the contrary, if another's stomach should turn at a sturgeon, wherein, I pray, is he happier than the other? If a man have a crooked, ill-favored wife, who yet in his eye may stand in competition with Venus, is it not the same as if she were truly beautiful? Or if seeing an ugly, ill-pointed piece, he should admire the work as believing it some great master's hand, were he not much happier, think you, than they that buy such things at vast rates, and yet perhaps reap less pleasure from them than the other? I know one of my name that gave his new married wife some counterfeit jewels, and as he was a pleasant droll, persuaded her that they were not only right but of an inestimable price; and what difference, I pray, to her, that was as well pleased and contented with glass and kept it as warily as if it had been a treasure? In the meantime the husband saved his money and had this advantage of her folly, that he obliged her as much as if he had bought them at a great rate. Or what difference, think you, between those in Plato's imaginary cave that stand gaping at the shadows and figures of things, so they please themselves and have no need to wish, and that wise man, who, being got loose from them, sees things truly as they are? Whereas that cobbler in Lucian if he might always have continued his golden dreams, he would never have desired any other happiness. So then there is no difference; or, if there be, the fools have the advantage: first, in that their happiness costs them least, that is to say, only some small persuasion; next, that they enjoy it in common. And the possession of no good can be delightful without a companion. For who does not know what a dearth there is of wise men, if yet any one be to be found? And though the Greeks for these so many ages have accounted upon seven only, yet so help me Hercules, do but examine them narrowly, and I'll be hanged if you find one half-witted fellow, nay or so much as one-quarter of a wise man, among them all.

For whereas among the many praises of Bacchus they reckon this the chief, that he washes away cares, and that too in an instant, do but sleep off his weak spirits, and they come on again, as we say, on horseback. But how much larger and more present is the benefit you receive by me, since, as it were with a perpetual drunkenness I fill your minds with mirth, fancies, and jollities, and that too without any trouble? Nor is there any man living whom I let be without it; whereas the gifts of the gods are scrambled, some to one and some to another. The sprightly delicious wine that drives away cares and leaves such a flavor behind it grows not everywhere. Beauty, the gift of Venus, happens to few; and to fewer gives Mercury eloquence. Hercules makes not everyone rich. Homer's Jupiter bestows not empire on all men. Mars oftentimes favors neither side. Many return sad from Apollo's oracle. Phoebus sometimes shoots a plague among us. Neptune drowns more than he saves: to say nothing of those mischievous gods, Plutoes, Ates, punishments, favors, and the like, not gods but executioners. I am that only Folly that so readily and indifferently bestows my benefits on all. Nor do I look to be entreated, or am I subject to take pet, and require an expiatory sacrifice if some ceremony be omitted. Nor do I beat heaven and earth together if, when the rest of the gods are invited, I am passed by or not admitted to the stream of their sacrifices. For the rest of the gods are so curious in this point that such an omission may chance to spoil a man's business; and therefore one has as good even let them alone as worship them: just like some men, who are so hard to please, and withall so ready to do mischief, that 'tis better be a stranger than have any familiarity with them.

But no man, you'll say, ever sacrificed to Folly or built me a temple. And troth, as I said before, I cannot but wonder at the ingratitude; yet because I am easily to be entreated, I take this also in good part, though truly I can scarce request it. For why should I require incense, wafers, a goat, or sow when all men pay me that worship everywhere which is so much approved even by our very divines? Unless perhaps I should envy Diana that her sacrifices are mingled with human blood. Then do I conceive myself most religiously worshiped when everywhere, as 'tis generally done, men embrace me in their minds, express me in their manners, and represent me in their lives, which worship of the saints is not so ordinary among Christians. How many are there that burn candles to the Virgin Mother, and that too at noonday when there's no need of them! But how few are there that study to imitate her in pureness of life, humility and love of heavenly things, which is the true worship and most acceptable to heaven! Besides why should I desire a temple when the whole world is my temple, and I'm deceived or 'tis a goodly one? Nor can I want priests but in a land where there are no men. Nor am I yet so foolish as to require statues or painted images, which do often obstruct my worship, since among the stupid and gross multitude those figures are worshiped for the saints themselves.

And so it would fare with me, as it does with them that are turned out of doors by their substitutes. No, I have statues enough, and as many as there are men, everyone bearing my lively resemblance in his face, how unwilling so ever he be to the contrary. And therefore there is no reason why I should envy the rest of the gods if in particular places they have their particular worship, and that too on set days—as Phoebus at Rhodes; at Cyprus, Venus; at Argos, Juno; at Athens, Minerva; in Olympus, Jupiter; at Tarentum, Neptune; and near the Hellespont, Priapus—as long as the world in general performs me every day much better sacrifices.

Wherein notwithstanding if I shall seem to anyone to have spoken more boldly than truly, let us, if you please, look a little into the lives of men, and it will easily appear not only how much they owe to me, but how much they esteem me even from the highest to the lowest. And yet we will not run over the lives of everyone, for that would be too long, but only some few of the great ones, from whence we shall easily conjecture the rest. For to what purpose is it to say anything of the common people, who without dispute are wholly mine? For they abound everywhere with so many several sorts of folly, and are every day so busy in inventing new, that a thousand Democriti are too few for so general a laughter, though there were another Democritus to laugh at them too. 'Tis almost incredible what sport and pastime they daily make the gods; for though they set aside their sober forenoon hours to dispatch business and receive prayers, yet when they begin to be well whittled with nectar and cannot think of anything that's serious, they get them up into some part of heaven that has better prospect than other and thence look down upon the actions of men. Nor is there anything that pleases them better. Good, good! what an excellent sight it is! How many several hurly-burlies of fools! for I myself sometimes sit among those poetical gods.

Here's one desperately in love with a young wench, and the more she slights him the more outrageously he loves her. Another marries a woman's money, not herself. Another's jealousy keeps more eyes on her than Argos. Another becomes a mourner, and how foolishly he carries it! nay, hires others to bear him company to make it more ridiculous. Another weeps over his mother-in-law's grave. Another spends all he can rap and run on his belly, to be the more hungry after it. Another thinks there is no happiness but in sleep and idleness. Another turmoils himself about other men's business and neglects his own. Another thinks himself rich in taking up moneys and changing securities, as we say borrowing of Peter to pay Paul, and in a short time becomes bankrupt. Another starves himself to enrich his heir. Another for a small and uncertain gain exposes his life to the casualties of seas and winds, which yet no money can restore. Another had rather get riches by war than live peaceably at home. And some there are that think them easiest attained by courting old childless men with presents; and others again by making rich old women believe they love them; both which afford the gods most excellent pastime, to see them cheated by those persons they thought to have over-caught. But the most foolish and basest of all others are our merchants, to wit such as venture on everything be it never so dishonest, and manage it no better; who though they lie by no allowance, swear and forswear, steal, cozen, and cheat, yet shuffle themselves into the first rank, and all because they have gold rings on their fingers. Nor are they without their flattering friars that admire them and give them openly the title of honorable, in hopes, no doubt, to get some small snip of it themselves.

There are also a kind of Pythagoreans with whom all things are so common that if they get anything under their cloaks, they make no more scruple of carrying it away than if it were their own by inheritance. There are others too that are only rich in conceit, and while they fancy to themselves pleasant dreams, conceive that enough to make them happy. Some desire to be accounted wealthy abroad and are yet ready to starve at home. One makes what haste he can to set all going, and another rakes it together by right or wrong. This man is ever laboring for public honors, and another lies sleeping in a chimney corner. A great many undertake endless suits and outvie one another who shall most enrich the dilatory judge or corrupt advocate. One is all for innovations and another for some great he-knows-not-what. Another leaves his wife and children at home and goes to Jerusalem, Rome, or in pilgrimage to St. James's where he has no business. In short, if a man like Menippus of old could look down from the moon and behold those innumerable rufflings of mankind, he would think he saw a swarm of flies and gnats quarreling among themselves, fighting, laying traps for one another, snatching, playing, wantoning, growing up, falling, and dying. Nor is it to be believed what stir, what broils, this little creature raises, and yet in how short a time it comes to nothing itself; while sometimes war, other times pestilence, sweeps off many thousands of them together.

But let me be most foolish myself, and one whom Democritus may not only laugh at but flout, if I go one foot further in the discovery of the follies and madnesses of the common people. I'll betake me to them that carry the reputation of wise men and hunt after that golden bough, as says the proverb. Among whom the grammarians hold the first place, a generation of men than whom nothing would be more miserable, nothing more perplexed, nothing more hated of the gods, did not I allay the troubles of that pitiful profession with a certain kind of pleasant madness. For they are not only subject to those five curses with which Home begins his Iliads, as says the Greek epigram, but six hundred; as being ever hunger-starved and slovens in their schools—schools, did I say? Nay, rather cloisters, bridewells, or slaughter-houses—grown old among a company of boys, deaf with their noise, and pined away with stench and nastiness. And yet by my courtesy it is that they think themselves the most excellent of all men, so greatly do they please themselves in frighting a company of fearful boys with a thundering voice and big looks, tormenting them with ferules, rods, and whips; and, laying about them without fear or wit, imitate the ass in the lion's skin. In the meantime all that nastiness seems absolute spruceness, that stench a perfume, and that miserable slavery a kingdom, and such too as they would not change their tyranny for Phalaris' or Dionysius' empire. Nor are they less

happy in that new opinion they have taken up of
being learned; for whereas most of them beat into
boys' heads nothing but foolish toys, yet, you good
gods! what Palemon, what Donatus, do they not
scorn in comparison of themselves? And so, I know
not by what tricks, they bring it about that to their
boys' foolish mothers and dolt-headed fathers they
pass for such as they fancy themselves. Add to this
that other pleasure of theirs, that if any of them happen to find out who was Anchises' mother, or pick
out of some worm-eaten manuscript a word not commonly known—as suppose it bubsequa for a cow-
herd, bovinator for a wrangler, manticulator for a
cutpurse—or dig up the ruins of some ancient monu-
ment with the letters half eaten out; O Jupiter! what
towerings! what triumphs! what commendations!
as if they had conquered Africa or taken in Babylon.

But what of this when they give up and down
their foolish insipid verses, and there wants not others that admire them as much? They believe presently that Virgil's soul is transmigrated into them!
But nothing like this, when with mutual compli-
ments they praise, admire, and claw one another.
Whereas if another do but slip a word and one more
quick-sighted than the rest discover it by accident, O
Hercules! what uproars, what bickerings, what
taunts, what invectives! If I lie, let me have the ill

will of all the grammarians. I knew in my time one of many arts, a Grecian, a Latinist, a mathematician, a philosopher, a physician, a man master of them all, and sixty years of age, who, laying by all the rest, perplexed and tormented himself for above twenty years in the study of grammar, fully reckoning himself a prince if he might but live so long till he could certainly determine how the eight parts of speech were to be distinguished, which none of the Greeks or Latins had yet fully cleared: as if it were a matter to be decided by the sword if a man made an adverb of a conjunction. And for this cause is it that we have as many grammars as grammarians; nay more, forasmuch as my friend Aldus has given us above five, not passing by any kind of grammar, how barbarously or tediously soever compiled, which he has not turned over and examined; envying every man's attempts in this kind, how to be pitied than happy, as persons that are ever tormenting themselves; adding, changing, putting in, blotting out, revising, reprinting, showing it to friends, and nine years in correcting, yet never fully satisfied; at so great a rate do they purchase this vain reward, to wit, praise, and that too of a very few, with so many watchings, so much sweat, so much vexation and loss of sleep, the most precious of all things. Add to this the waste of health, spoil of complexion, weakness of eyes or rather blindness, poverty, envy, abstinence from pleasure, over-hasty old age, untimely death, and the like; so highly does this wise man value the approbation of one or two blear-eyed fellows. But how much happier is this my writer's dotage who never studies for anything but puts in writing whatever he pleases or what comes first in his head, though it be but his dreams; and all this with small waste of paper, as well knowing that the vainer those trifles are, the higher esteem they will have with the greater number, that is to say all the fools and unlearned. And what matter is it to slight those few learned if yet they ever read them? Or of what authority will the censure of so few wise men be against so great a cloud of gainsayers?

But they are the wiser that put out other men's works for their own, and transfer that glory which others with great pains have obtained to themselves; relying on this, that they conceive, though it should so happen that their theft be never so plainly detected, that yet they should enjoy the pleasure of it for the present. And 'tis worth one's while to consider how they please themselves when they are applauded by the common people, pointed at in a crowd, "This is that excellent person;" lie on booksellers' stalls; and in the top of every page have three hard words read, but chiefly exotic and next degree to conjuring;

which, by the immortal gods! what are they but
mere words? And again, if you consider the world,
by how few understood, and praised by fewer! for
even among the unlearned there are different palates.
Or what is it that their own very names are often
counterfeit or borrowed from some books of the ancients? When one styles himself Telemachus, another Sthenelus, a third Laertes, a fourth Polycrates,
a fifth Thrasymachus. So that there is no difference
whether they title their books with the "Tale of a
Tub," or, according to the philosophers, by alpha,
beta.

But the most pleasant of all is to see them praise
one another with reciprocal epistles, verses, and en-
comiums; fools their fellow fools, and dunces their
brother dunces. This, in the other's opinion, is an
absolute Alcaeus; and the other, in his, a very Cal-
limachus. He looks upon Tully as nothing to the
other, and the other again pronounces him more
learned than Plato. And sometimes too they pick out
their antagonist and think to raise themselves a fame
by writing one against the other; while the giddy
multitude are so long divided to whether of the two
they shall determine the victory, till each goes off
conqueror, and, as if he had done some great action,
fancies himself a triumph. And now wise men laugh
at these things as foolish, as indeed they are. Who

denies it? Yet in the meantime, such is my kindness to them, they live a merry life and would not change their imaginary triumphs, no, not with the Scipioes. While yet those learned men, though they laugh their fill and reap the benefit of the other's folly, cannot without ingratitude deny but that even they too are not a little beholding to me themselves.

And among them our advocates challenge the first place, nor is there any sort of people that please themselves like them: for while they daily roll Sisyphus his stone, and quote you a thousand cases, as it were, in a breath no matter how little to the purpose, and heap glosses upon glosses, and opinions on the neck of opinions, they bring it at last to this pass, that that study of all other seems the most difficult. Add to these our logicians and sophists, a generation of men more prattling than an echo and the worst of them able to outchat a hundred of the best picked gossips. And yet their condition would be much better were they only full of words and not so given to scolding that they most obstinately hack and hew one another about a matter of nothing and make such a sputter about terms and words till they have quite lost the sense. And yet they are so happy in the good opinion of themselves that as soon as they are furnished with two or three syllogisms, they dare boldly enter the lists against any man upon any point, as not doubting but to run him down with noise, though the opponent were another Stentor.

And next these come our philosophers, so much reverenced for their furred gowns and starched beards that they look upon themselves as the only wise men and all others as shadows. And yet how pleasantly do they dote while they frame in their heads innumerable worlds; measure out the sun, the moon, the stars, nay and heaven itself, as it were, with a pair of compasses; lay down the causes of lightning, winds, eclipses, and other the like inexplicable matters; and all this too without the least doubting, as if they were Nature's secretaries, or dropped down among us from the council of the gods; while in the meantime Nature laughs at them and all their blind conjectures. For that they know nothing, even this is a sufficient argument, that they don't agree among themselves and so are incomprehensible touching every particular. These, though they have not the least degree of knowledge, profess yet that they have mastered all; nay, though they neither know themselves, nor perceive a ditch or block that lies in their way, for that perhaps most of them are half blind, or their wits a wool-gathering, yet give out that they have discovered ideas, universalities, separated forms, first matters, quiddities, haecceities, formalities, and the like stuff; things so thin and bodiless that I believe even Lynceus himself was not able to perceive them. But then chiefly do they disdain the unhallowed crowd as often as with their triangles, quadrangles, circles, and the like mathematical devices, more confounded than a labyrinth, and letters disposed one against the other, as it were in battle array, they cast a mist before the eyes of the ignorant. Nor is there wanting of this kind some that pretend to foretell things by the stars and make promises of miracles beyond all things of soothsaying, and are so fortunate as to meet with people that believe them.

But perhaps I had better pass over our divines in silence and not stir this pool or touch this fair but unsavory plant, as a kind of men that are supercilious beyond comparison, and to that too, implacable; lest setting them about my ears, they attack me by troops and force me to a recantation sermon, which if I refuse, they straight pronounce me a heretic. For this is the thunderbolt with which they fright those whom they are resolved not to favor. And truly, though there are few others that less willingly acknowledge the kindnesses I have done them, yet even these too stand fast bound to me upon no ordinary accounts; while being happy in their own opinion, and as if they dwelt in the third heaven, they look with haughtiness on all others as poor creeping

things and could almost find in their hearts to pity
them; while hedged in with so many magisterial defi-
nitions, conclusions, corollaries, propositions explicit
and implicit, they abound with so many starting-holes
that Vulcan's net cannot hold them so fast, but they'll
slip through with their distinctions, with which they
so easily cut all knots asunder that a hatchet could
not have done it better, so plentiful are they in their
new-found words and prodigious terms. Besides,
while they explicate the most hidden mysteries according to their own fancy—as how the world was
first made; how original sin is derived to posterity;
in what manner, how much room, and how long
time Christ lay in the Virgin's womb; how accidents
subsist in the Eucharist without their subject.

But these are common and threadbare; these are
worthy of our great and illuminated divines, as the
world calls them! At these, if ever they fall athwart
them, they prick up—as whether there was any instant of time in the generation of the Second Person;
whether there be more than one filiation in Christ;
whether it be a possible proposition that God the
Father hates the Son; or whether it was possible that
Christ could have taken upon Him the likeness of a
woman, or of the devil, or of an ass, or of a stone, or
of a gourd; and then how that gourd should have
preached, wrought miracles, or been hung on the

cross; and what Peter had consecrated if he had administered the Sacrament at what time the body of
Christ hung upon the cross; or whether at the same
time he might be said to be man; whether after the
Resurrection there will be any eating and drinking,
since we are so much afraid of hunger and thirst in
this world. There are infinite of these subtle trifles,
and others more subtle than these, of notions, rela-
tions, instants, formalities, quiddities, haecceities,
which no one can perceive without a Lynceus whose
eyes could look through a stone wall and discover
those things through the thickest darkness that never
were.

Add to this those their other determinations, and
those too so contrary to common opinion that those
oracles of the Stoics, which they call paradoxes, seem
in comparison of these but blockish and idle—as 'tis
a lesser crime to kill a thousand men than to set a
stitch on a poor man's shoe on the Sabbath day; and
that a man should rather choose that the whole world
with all food and raiment, as they say, should perish,
than tell a lie, though never so inconsiderable. And
these most subtle subtleties are rendered yet more
subtle by the several methods of so many Schoolmen, that one might sooner wind himself out of a
labyrinth than the entanglements of the realists,
nominalists, Thomists, Albertists, Occamists, Scot-

ists. Nor have I named all the several sects, but only some of the chief; in all which there is so much doctrine and so much difficulty that I may well conceive the apostles, had they been to deal with these new kind of divines, had needed to have prayed in aid of some other spirit.

Paul knew what faith was, and yet when he said, "Faith is the substance of things hoped for, and the evidence of things not seen," he did not define it doctor-like. And as he understood charity well himself, so he did as illogically divide and define it to others in his first Epistle to the Corinthians, Chapter the thirteenth. And devoutly, no doubt, did the apostles consecrate the Eucharist; yet, had they been asked the question touching the "terminus a quo" and the "terminus ad quem" of transubstantiation; of the manner how the same body can be in several places at one and the same time; of the difference the body of Christ has in heaven from that of the cross, or this in the Sacrament; in what point of time transubstantiation is, whereas prayer, by means of which it is, as being a discrete quantity, is transient; they would not, I conceive, have answered with the same subtlety as the Scotists dispute and define it. They knew the mother of Jesus, but which of them has so philosophically demonstrated how she was preserved from original sin as have done our divines?

Peter received the keys, and from Him too that would not have trusted them with a person unworthy; yet whether he had understanding or no, I know not, for certainly he never attained to that subtlety to determine how he could have the key of knowledge that had no knowledge himself. They baptized far and near, and yet taught nowhere what was the formal, material, efficient, and final cause of baptism, nor made the least mention of delible and indelible characters. They worshiped, 'tis true, but in spirit, following herein no other than that of the Gospel, "God is a Spirit, and they that worship, must worship him in spirit and truth;" yet it does not appear it was at that time revealed to them that an image sketched on the wall with a coal was to be worshiped with the same worship as Christ Himself, if at least the two forefingers be stretched out, the hair long and uncut, and have three rays about the crown of the head. For who can conceive these things, unless he has spent at least six and thirty years in the philosophical and supercelestial whims of Aristotle and the Schoolmen?

In like manner, the apostles press to us grace; but which of them distinguishes between free grace and grace that makes a man acceptable? They exhort us to good works, and yet determine not what is the work working, and what a resting in the work done.

They incite us to charity, and yet make no difference between charity infused and charity wrought in us by our own endeavors. Nor do they declare whether it be an accident or a substance, a thing created or uncreated. They detest and abominate sin, but let me not live if they could define according to art what that is which we call sin, unless perhaps they were inspired by the spirit of the Scotists. Nor can I be brought to believe that Paul, by whose learning you may judge the rest, would have so often condemned questions, disputes, genealogies, and, as himself calls them, "strifes of words," if he had thoroughly understood those subtleties, especially when all the debates and controversies of those times were rude and blockish in comparison of the more than Chrysippean subtleties of our masters. Although yet the gentlemen are so modest that if they meet with anything written by the apostles not so smooth and even as might be expected from a master, they do not presently condemn it but handsomely bend it to their own purpose, so great respect and honor do they give, partly to antiquity and partly to the name of apostle. And truly 'twas a kind of injustice to require so great things of them that never heard the least word from their masters concerning it. And so if the like happen in Chrysostom, Basil, Jerome, they think it enough to say they are not obliged by it.

The apostles also confuted the heathen philosophers and Jews, a people than whom none more
obstinate, but rather by their good lives and miracles
than syllogisms: and yet there was scarce one among
them that was capable of understanding the least
"quodlibet" of the Scotists. But now, where is that
heathen or heretic that must not presently stoop to
such wire-drawn subtleties, unless he be so thick-
skulled that he can't apprehend them, or so impudent as to hiss them down, or, being furnished with
the same tricks, be able to make his party good with
them? As if a man should set a conjurer on work
against a conjurer, or fight with one hallowed sword
against another, which would prove no other than a
work to no purpose. For my own part I conceive the
Christians would do much better if instead of those
dull troops and companies of soldiers with which
they have managed their war with such doubtful
success, they would send the bawling Scotists, the
most obstinate Occamists, and invincible Albertists
to war against the Turks and Saracens; and they
would see, I guess, a most pleasant combat and such
a victory as was never before. For who is so faint
whom their devices will not enliven? who so stupid
whom such spurs can't quicken? or who so quick-
sighted before whose eyes they can't cast a mist?

But you'll say, I jest. Nor are you without cause,
since even among divines themselves there are some

that have learned better and are ready to turn their
stomachs at those foolish subtleties of the others.
There are some that detest them as a kind of sacrilege and count it the height of impiety to speak so
irreverently of such hidden things, rather to be
adored than explicated; to dispute of them with such
profane and heathenish niceties; to define them so
arrogantly and pollute the majesty of divinity with
such pithless and sordid terms and opinions. Meantime the others please, nay hug themselves in their
happiness, and are so taken up with these pleasant
trifles that they have not so much leisure as to cast
the least eye on the Gospel or St. Paul's epistles. And
while they play the fool at this rate in their schools,
they make account the universal church would otherwise perish, unless, as the poets fancied of Atlas that
he supported heaven with his shoulders, they under-
propped the other with their syllogistical buttresses.
And how great a happiness is this, think you? while,
as if Holy Writ were a nose of wax, they fashion and
refashion it according to their pleasure; while they
require that their own conclusions, subscribed by two
or three Schoolmen, be accounted greater than Solon's laws and preferred before the papal decretals;
while, as censors of the world, they force everyone
to a recantation that differs but a hair's breadth from
the least of their explicit or implicit determinations.

And those too they pronounce like oracles. This proposition is scandalous; this irreverent; this has a smack of heresy; this no very good sound: so that neither baptism, nor the Gospel, nor Paul, nor Peter, nor St. Jerome, nor St. Augustine, no nor most Aristotelian Thomas himself can make a man a Christian, without these bachelors too be pleased to give him his grace. And the like in their subtlety in judging; for who would think he were no Christian that should say these two speeches "matula putes" and "matula putet," or "ollae fervere" and "ollam fervere" were not both good Latin, unless their wisdoms had taught us the contrary? who had delivered the church from such mists of error, which yet no one ever met with, had they not come out with some university seal for it? And are they not most happy while they do these things?

Then for what concerns hell, how exactly they describe everything, as if they had been conversant in that commonwealth most part of their time! Again, how do they frame in their fancy new orbs, adding to those we have already an eighth! a goodly one, no doubt, and spacious enough, lest perhaps their happy souls might lack room to walk in, entertain their friends, and now and then play at football. And with these and a thousand the like fopperies their heads are so full stuffed and stretched that I believe Jupiter's brain was not near so big when, being in labor with Pallas, he was beholding to the midwifery of Vulcan's axe. And therefore you must not wonder if in their public disputes they are so bound about the head, lest otherwise perhaps their brains might leap out. Nay, I have sometimes laughed myself to see them so tower in their own opinion when they speak most barbarously; and when they humh and hawh so pitifully that none but one of their own tribe can understand them, they call it heights which the vulgar can't reach; for they say 'tis beneath the dignity of divine mysteries to be cramped and tied up to the narrow rules of grammarians: from whence we may conjecture the great prerogative of divines, if they only have the privilege of speaking corruptly, in which yet every cobbler thinks himself concerned for his share. Lastly, they look upon themselves as somewhat more than men as often as they are devoutly saluted by the name of "Our Masters," in which they fancy there lies as much as in the Jews' "Jehovah;" and therefore they reckon it a crime if "Magister Noster" be written other than in capital letters; and if anyone should preposterously say "Noster Magister," he has at once overturned the whole body of divinity.

And next these come those that commonly call themselves the religious and monks, most false in both titles, when both a great part of them are farthest from religion, and no men swarm thicker in all places than themselves. Nor can I think of anything that could be more miserable did not I support them so many several ways. For whereas all men detest them to that height, that they take it for ill luck to meet one of them by chance, yet such is their happiness that they flatter themselves. For first, they reckon it one of the main points of piety if they are so illiterate that they can't so much as read. And then when they run over their offices, which they carry about them, rather by tale than understanding, they believe the gods more than ordinarily pleased with their braying. And some there are among them that put off their trumperies at vast rates, yet rove up and down for the bread they eat; nay, there is scarce an inn, wagon, or ship into which they intrude not, to the no small damage of the commonwealth of beggars. And yet, like pleasant fellows, with all this vileness, ignorance, rudeness, and impudence, they represent to us, for so they call it, the lives of the apostles. Yet what is more pleasant than that they do all things by rule and, as it were, a kind of mathematics, the least swerving from which were a crime beyond forgiveness—as how many knots their shoes must be tied with, of what color everything is, what distinction of habits, of what stuff made, how

many straws broad their girdles and of what fashion,
how many bushels wide their cowl, how many fingers long their hair, and how many hours sleep;
which exact equality, how disproportionate it is,
among such variety of bodies and tempers, who is
there that does not perceive it? And yet by reason
of these fooleries they not only set slight by others,
but each different order, men otherwise professing
apostolical charity, despise one another, and for the
different wearing of a habit, or that 'tis of darker
color, they put all things in combustion. And among
these there are some so rigidly religious that their
upper garment is haircloth, their inner of the finest
linen; and, on the contrary, others wear linen without and hair next their skins. Others, again, are as
afraid to touch money as poison, and yet neither forbear wine nor dallying with women. In a word, 'tis
their only care that none of them come near one another in their manner of living, nor do they endeavor
how they may be like Christ, but how they may
differ among themselves.

And another great happiness they conceive in
their names, while they call themselves Cordiliers,
and among these too, some are Colletes, some Minors, some Minims, some Crossed; and again, these
are Benedictines, those Bernardines; these Carmel-
ites, those Augustines; these Williamites, and those

Jacobines; as if it were not worth the while to be called Christians. And of these, a great part build so much on their ceremonies and petty traditions of men that they think one heaven is too poor a reward for so great merit, little dreaming that the time will come when Christ, not regarding any of these trifles, will call them to account for His precept of charity. One shall show you a large trough full of all kinds of fish; another tumble you out so many bushels of prayers; another reckon you so many myriads of fasts, and fetch them up again in one dinner by eating till he cracks again; another produces more bundles of ceremonies than seven of the stoutest ships would be able to carry; another brags he has not touched a penny these three score years without two pair of gloves at least upon his hands; another wears a cowl so lined with grease that the poorest tarpaulin would not stoop to take it up; another will tell you he has lived these fifty-five years like a sponge, continually fastened to the same place; another is grown hoarse with his daily chanting; another has contracted a lethargy by his solitary living; and another the palsy in his tongue for want of speaking. But Christ, interrupting them in their vanities, which otherwise were endless, will ask them, "Whence this new kind of Jews? I acknowledge one commandment, which is truly mine, of which alone I hear nothing. I promised, 'tis true, my Father's heritage, and that without parables, not to cowls, odd prayers, and fastings, but to the duties of faith and charity. Nor can I acknowledge them that least acknowledge their faults. They that would seem holier than myself, let them if they like possess to themselves those three hundred sixty-five heavens of Basilides the heretic's invention, or command them whose foolish traditions they have preferred before my precepts to erect them a new one." When they shall hear these things and see common ordinary persons preferred before them, with what countenance, think you, will they behold one another? In the meantime they are happy in their hopes, and for this also they are beholding to me.

And yet these kind of people, though they are as it were of another commonwealth, no man dares despise, especially those begging friars, because they are privy to all men's secrets by means of confessions, as they call them. Which yet were no less than treason to discover, unless, being got drunk, they have a mind to be pleasant, and then all comes out, that is to say by hints and conjectures but suppressing the names. But if anyone should anger these wasps, they'll sufficiently revenge themselves in their public sermons and so point out their enemy by circumlocutions that there's no one but understands whom 'tis they mean, unless he understand nothing at all; nor will they give over their barking till you throw the dogs a bone. And now tell me, what juggler or mountebank you had rather behold than hear them rhetorically play the fool in their preachments, and yet most sweetly imitating what rhetoricians have written touching the art of good speaking? Good God! what several postures they have! How they shift their voice, sing out their words, skip up and down, and are ever and anon making such new faces that they confound all things with noise! And yet this knack of theirs is no less a mystery that runs in succession from one brother to another; which though it be not lawful for me to know, however I'll venture at it by conjectures. And first they invoke whatever they have scraped from the poets; and in the next place, if they are to discourse of charity, they take their rise from the river Nilus; or to set out the mystery of the cross, from bell and the dragon; or to dispute of fasting, from the twelve signs of the zodiac; or, being to preach of faith, ground their matter on the square of a circle.

I have heard myself one, and he no small fool—I was mistaken, I would have said scholar—that being in a famous assembly explaining the mystery of the Trinity, that he might both let them see his learning was not ordinary and withal satisfy some theological ears, he took a new way, to wit from the letters, syllables, and the word itself; then from the coherence of the nominative case and the verb, and the adjective and substantive: and while most of the audience wondered, and some of them muttered that of Horace, "What does all this trumpery drive at?" at last he brought the matter to this head, that he would demonstrate that the mystery of the Trinity was so clearly expressed in the very rudiments of grammar that the best mathematician could not chalk it out more plainly. And in this discourse did this most superlative theologian beat his brains for eight whole months that at this hour he's as blind as a beetle, to wit, all the sight of his eyes being run into the sharpness of his wit. But for all that he thinks nothing of his blindness, rather taking the same for too cheap a price of such a glory as he won thereby.

And besides him I met with another, some eighty years of age, and such a divine that you'd have sworn Scotus himself was revived in him. He, being upon the point of unfolding the mystery of the name Jesus, did with wonderful subtlety demonstrate that there lay hidden in those letters whatever could be said of him; for that it was only declined with three cases, he said, it was a manifest token of the Divine Trinity; and then, that the first ended in *S,* the sec-

ond in *M*, the third in *U*, there was in it an ineffable
mystery, to wit, those three letters declaring to us
that he was the beginning, middle, and end (*sum-
mum, medium, et ultimum*) of all. Nay, the mystery was yet more abstruse; for he so mathematically
split the word Jesus into two equal parts that he left
the middle letter by itself, and then told us that that
letter in Hebrew was *schin* or *sin,* and that *sin* in the
Scotch tongue, as he remembered, signified as much
as sin; from whence he gathered that it was Jesus
that took away the sins of the world. At which new
exposition the audience were so wonderfully intent
and struck with admiration, especially the theologians, that there wanted little but that Niobe-like
they had been turned to stones; whereas the like had
almost happened to me, as befell the Priapus in Horace. And not without cause, for when were the
Grecian Demosthenes or Roman Cicero ever guilty
of the like? They thought that introduction faulty
that was wide of the matter, as if it were not the way
of carters and swineherds that have no more wit
than God sent them. But these learned men think
their preamble, for so they call it, then chiefly rhetor-
ical when it has least coherence with the rest of the
argument, that the admiring audience may in the
meanwhile whisper to themselves, "What will he be
at now?" In the third place, they bring in instead of

narration some texts of Scripture, but handle them cursorily, and as it were by the bye, when yet it is the only thing they should have insisted on. And fourthly, as it were changing a part in the play, they bolt out with some question in divinity, and many times relating neither to earth nor heaven, and this they look upon as a piece of art. Here they erect their theological crests and beat into the people's ears those magnificent titles of illustrious doctors, subtle doctors, most subtle doctors, seraphic doctors, cherubin doctors, holy doctors, unquestionable doctors, and the like; and then throw abroad among the ignorant people syllogisms, majors, minors, conclusions, corollaries, suppositions, and those so weak and foolish that they are below pedantry. There remains yet the fifth act in which one would think they should show their mastery. And here they bring in some foolish insipid fable out of *Speculum Historiale* or *Gesta Romanorum* and expound it allegorically, tropologically, and anagogically. And after this manner do they and their chimera, and such as Horace despaired of compassing when he wrote "Humano capiti," etc.

But they have heard from somebody, I know not whom, that the beginning of a speech should be sober and grave and least given to noise. And therefore they begin theirs at that rate they can scarce hear themselves, as if it were not matter whether anyone understood them. They have learned somewhere that to move the affections a louder voice is requisite. Whereupon they that otherwise would speak like a mouse in a cheese start out of a sudden into a downright fury, even there too, where there's the least need of it. A man would swear they were past the power of hellebore, so little do they consider where 'tis they run out. Again, because they have heard that as a speech comes up to something, a man should press it more earnestly, they, however they begin, use a strange contention of voice in every part, though the matter itself be never so flat, and end in that manner as if they'd run themselves out of breath. Lastly, they have learned that among rhetoricians there is some mention of laughter, and therefore they study to prick in a jest here and there; but, O Venus! so void of wit and so little to the purpose that it may be truly called an ass's playing on the harp. And sometimes also they use somewhat of a sting, but so nevertheless that they rather tickle than wound; nor do they ever more truly flatter than when they would seem to use the greatest freedom of speech. Lastly, such is their whole action that a man would swear they had learned it from our common tumblers, though yet they come short of them in every respect. However, they are both so like that no man will dispute but that either these learned their rhetoric from them, or they theirs from these. And yet they light on some that, when they hear them, conceive they hear very Demosthenes and Ciceroes: of which sort chiefly are our merchants and women, whose ears only they endeavor to please, because as to the first, if they stroke them handsomely, some part or other of their ill-gotten goods is wont to fall to their share. And the women, though for many other things they favor this order, this is not the least, that they commit to their breasts whatever discontents they have against their husbands. And now, I conceive me, you see how much this kind of people are beholding to me, that with their petty ceremonies, ridiculous trifles, and noise exercise a kind of tyranny among mankind, believing themselves very Pauls and Anthonies.

But I willingly give over these stage-players that are such ingrateful dissemblers of the courtesies I have done them and such impudent pretenders to religion which they haven't. And now I have a mind to give some small touches of princes and courts, of whom I am had in reverence, aboveboard and, as it becomes gentlemen, frankly. And truly, if they had the least proportion of sound judgment, what life were more unpleasant than theirs, or so much to be avoided? For whoever did but truly weigh with himself how great a burden lies upon his shoulders that would truly discharge the duty of a prince, he would not think it worth his while to make his way to a crown by perjury and parricide. He would consider that he that takes a scepter in his hand should manage the public, not his private, interest; study nothing but the common good; and not in the least go contrary to those laws whereof himself is both the author and exactor: that he is to take an account of the good or evil administration of all his magistrates and subordinate officers; that, though he is but one, all men's eyes are upon him, and in his power it is, either like a good planet to give life and safety to mankind by his harmless influence, or like a fatal comet to send mischief and destruction; that the vices of other men are not alike felt, nor so generally communicated; and that a prince stands in that place that his least deviation from the rule of honesty and honor reaches farther than himself and opens a gap to many men's ruin. Besides, that the fortune of princes has many things attending it that are but too apt to train them out of the way, as pleasure, liberty, flattery, excess; for which cause he should the more diligently endeavor and set a watch over himself, lest perhaps he be led aside and fail in his duty. Lastly, to say nothing of treasons, ill will, and such other mischiefs he's in jeopardy of, that that

True King is over his head, who in a short time will call him to account for every the least trespass, and that so much the more severely by how much more mighty was the empire committed to his charge. These and the like if a prince should duly weigh, and weigh it he would if he were wise, he would neither be able to sleep nor take any hearty repast.

But now by my courtesy they leave all this care to the gods and are only taken up with themselves, not admitting anyone to their ear but such as know how to speak pleasant things and not trouble them with business. They believe they have discharged all the duty of a prince if they hunt every day, keep a stable of fine horses, sell dignities and commanderies, and invent new ways of draining the citizens' purses and bringing it into their own exchequer; but under such dainty new-found names that though the thing be most unjust in itself, it carries yet some face of equity; adding to this some little sweet'nings that whatever happens, they may be secure of the common people. And now suppose someone, such as they sometimes are, a man ignorant of laws, little less than an enemy to the public good, and minding nothing but his own, given up to pleasure, a hater of learning, liberty, and justice, studying nothing less than the public safety, but measuring everything by his own will and profit; and then put on him a golden chain that declares the accord of all virtues linked one to another; a crown set with diamonds, that should put him in mind how he ought to excel all others in heroic virtues; besides a scepter, the emblem of justice and an untainted heart; and lastly, a purple robe, a badge of that charity he owes the commonwealth. All which if a prince should compare them with his own life, he would, I believe, be clearly ashamed of his bravery, and be afraid lest some or other gibing expounder turn all this tragical furniture into a ridiculous laughingstock.

And as to the court lords, what should I mention them? than most of whom though there be nothing more indebted, more servile, more witless, more contemptible, yet they would seem as they were the most excellent of all others. And yet in this only thing no men more modest, in that they are contented to wear about them gold, jewels, purple, and those other marks of virtue and wisdom; but for the study of the things themselves, they remit it to others, thinking it happiness enough for them that they can call the king master, have learned the cringe *à la mode,* know when and where to use those titles of Your Grace, My Lord, Your Magnificence; in a word that they are past all shame and can flatter pleasantly. For these are the arts that speak a man truly noble and an exact courtier. But if you look into their manner of life you'll find them mere sots, as debauched as Penelope's wooers; you know the other part of the verse, which the echo will better tell you than I can. They sleep till noon and have their mercenary Levite come to their bedside, where he chops over his matins before they are half up. Then to breakfast, which is scarce done but dinner stays for them. From thence they go to dice, tables, cards, or entertain themselves with jesters, fools, gambols, and horse tricks. In the meantime they have one or two beverages, and then supper, and after that a banquet, and 'twere well, by Jupiter, there were no more than one. And in this manner do their hours, days, months, years, age slide away without the least irksomeness. Nay, I have sometimes gone away many inches fatter, to see them speak big words; while each of the ladies believes herself so much nearer to the gods by how much the longer train she trails after her; while one nobleman edges out another, that he may get the nearer to Jupiter himself; and everyone of them pleases himself the more by how much more massive is the chain he swags on his shoulders, as if he meant to show his strength as well as his wealth.

Nor are princes by themselves in their manner of life, since popes, cardinals, and bishops have so diligently followed their steps that they've almost got

the start of them. For if any of them would consider
what their Albe should put them in mind of, to wit
a blameless life; what is meant by their forked mi-
ters, whose each point is held in by the same knot,
we'll suppose it a perfect knowledge of the Old and
New Testaments; what those gloves on their hands,
but a sincere administration of the Sacraments, and
free from all touch of worldly business; what their
crosier, but a careful looking after the flock committed to their charge; what the cross born before them,
but victory over all earthly affections—these, I say,
and many of the like kind should anyone truly consider, would he not live a sad and troublesome life?
Whereas now they do well enough while they feed
themselves only, and for the care of their flock either
put it over to Christ or lay it all on their suffragans,
as they call them, or some poor vicars. Nor do they
so much as remember their name, or what the word
bishop signifies, to wit, labor, care, and trouble. But
in racking to gather money they truly act the part of
bishops, and herein acquit themselves to be no blind
seers.

In like manner cardinals, if they thought themselves the successors of the apostles, they would likewise imagine that the same things the other did are
required of them, and that they are not lords but dis-
pensers of spiritual things of which they must shortly

give an exact account. But if they also would a little philosophize on their habit and think with themselves what's the meaning of their linen rochet, is it not a remarkable and singular integrity of life? What that inner purple; is it not an earnest and fervent love of God? Or what that outward, whose loose plaits and long train fall round his Reverence's mule and are large enough to cover a camel; is it not charity that spreads itself so wide to the succor of all men? that is, to instruct, exhort, comfort, reprehend, admonish, compose wars, resist wicked princes, and willingly expend not only their wealth but their very lives for the flock of Christ: though yet what need at all of wealth to them that supply the room of the poor apostles? These things, I say, did they but duly consider, they would not be so ambitious of that dignity; or, if they were, they would willingly leave it and live a laborious, careful life, such as was that of the ancient apostles.

And for popes, that supply the place of Christ, if they should endeavor to imitate His life, to wit His poverty, labor, doctrine, cross, and contempt of life, or should they consider what the name pope, that is father, or holiness, imports, who would live more disconsolate than themselves? or who would purchase that chair with all his substance? or defend it, so purchased, with swords, poisons, and all force imaginable? so great a profit would the access of wisdom deprive him of—wisdom did I say? nay, the least corn of that salt which Christ speaks of: so much wealth, so much honor, so much riches, so many victories, so many offices, so many dispensations, so much tribute, so many pardons; such horses, such mules, such guards, and so much pleasure would it lose them. You see how much I have comprehended in a little: instead of which it would bring in watchings, fastings, tears, prayers, sermons, good endeavors, sighs, and a thousand the like troublesome exercises. Nor is this least considerable: so many scribes, so many copying clerks, so many notaries, so many advocates, so many promoters, so many secretaries, so many muleteers, so many grooms, so many bankers: in short, that vast multitude of men that overcharge the Roman See—I mistook, I meant honor—might beg their bread.

A most inhuman and economical thing, and more to be execrated, that those great princes of the Church and true lights of the world should be reduced to a staff and a wallet. Whereas now, if there be anything that requires their pains, they leave that to Peter and Paul that have leisure enough; but if there be anything of honor or pleasure, they take that to themselves. By which means it is, yet by my courtesy, that scarce any kind of men live more voluptuously or with less trouble; as believing that Christ will be well enough pleased if in their mystical and almost mimical pontificality, ceremonies, titles of holiness and the like, and blessing and cursing, they play the parts of bishops. To work miracles is old and antiquated, and not in fashion now; to instruct the people, troublesome; to interpret the Scripture, pedantic; to pray, a sign one has little else to do; to shed tears, silly and womanish; to be poor, base; to be vanquished, dishonorable and little becoming him that scarce admits even kings to kiss his slipper; and lastly, to die, uncouth; and to be stretched on a cross, infamous.

Theirs are only those weapons and sweet blessings which Paul mentions, and of these truly they are bountiful enough: as interdictions, hangings, heavy burdens, reproofs, anathemas, executions in effigy, and that terrible thunderbolt of excommunication, with the very sight of which they sink men's souls beneath the bottom of hell: which yet these most holy fathers in Christ and His vicars hurl with more fierceness against none than against such as, by the instigation of the devil, attempt to lessen or rob them of Peter's patrimony. When, though those words in the Gospel, "We have left all, and followed Thee," were his, yet they call his patrimony lands, cities, tribute, imposts, riches; for which, being enflamed

with the love of Christ, they contend with fire and
sword, and not without loss of much Christian blood,
and believe they have then most apostolically de-
fended the Church, the spouse of Christ, when the
enemy, as they call them, are valiantly routed. As
if the Church had any deadlier enemies than wicked
prelates, who not only suffer Christ to run out of request for want of preaching him, but hinder his
spreading by their multitudes of laws merely con-
trived for their own profit, corrupt him by their
forced expositions, and murder him by the evil example of their pestilent life.

Nay, further, whereas the Church of Christ was
founded in blood, confirmed by blood, and aug-
mented by blood, now, as if Christ, who after his
wonted manner defends his people, were lost, they
govern all by the sword. And whereas war is so sav-
age a thing that it rather befits beasts than men, so
outrageous that the very poets feigned it came from
the Furies, so pestilent that it corrupts all men's
manners, so unjust that it is best executed by the
worst of men, so wicked that it has no agreement
with Christ; and yet, omitting all the other, they
make this their only business. Here you'll see decrepit old fellows acting the parts of young men,
neither troubled at their costs, nor wearied with their
labors, nor discouraged at anything, so they may

have the liberty of turning laws, religion, peace, and all things else quite topsy-turvy. Nor are they destitute of their learned flatterers that call that palpable madness zeal, piety, and valor, having found out a new way by which a man may kill his brother without the least breach of that charity which, by the command of Christ, one Christian owes another. And here, in troth, I'm a little at a stand whether the ecclesiastical German electors gave them this example, or rather took it from them; who, laying aside their habit, benedictions, and all the like ceremonies, so act the part of commanders that they think it a mean thing, and least beseeming a bishop, to show the least courage to Godward unless it be in a battle.

And as to the common herd of priests, they account it a crime to degenerate from the sanctity of their prelates. Heidah! How soldier-like they bustle about the *jus divinum* of titles, and how quick-sighted they are to pick the least thing out of the writings of the ancients wherewith they may fright the common people and convince them, if possible, that more than a tenth is due! Yet in the meantime it least comes in their heads how many things are everywhere extant concerning that duty which they owe the people. Nor does their shorn crown in the least admonish them that a priest should be free from all worldly desires and think of nothing but heavenly things. Whereas on the contrary, these jolly fellows say they have sufficiently discharged their offices if they but anyhow mumble over a few odd prayers, which, so help me, Hercules! I wonder if any god either hear or understand, since they do neither themselves, especially when they thunder them out in that manner they are wont. But this they have in common with those of the heathens, that they are vigilant enough to the harvest of their profit, nor is there any of them that is not better read in those laws than the Scripture. Whereas if there be anything burdensome, they prudently lay that on other men's shoulders and shift it from one to the other, as men toss a ball from hand to hand, following herein the example of lay princes who commit the government of their kingdoms to their grand ministers, and they again to others, and leave all study of piety to the common people. In like manner the common people put it over to those they call ecclesiastics, as if themselves were no part of the Church, or that their vow in baptism had lost its obligation. Again, the priests that call themselves secular, as if they were initiated to the world, not to Christ, lay the burden on the regulars; the regulars on the monks; the monks that have more liberty on those that have less; and all of them on the mendicants; the mendicants on the Carthusians, among whom, if anywhere, this piety lies buried, but yet so close that scarce anyone can perceive it. In like manner the popes, the most diligent of all others in gathering in the harvest of money, refer all their apostolical work to the bishops, the bishops to the parsons, the parsons to the vicars, the vicars to their brother mendicants, and they again throw back the care of the flock on those that take the wool.

But it is not my business to sift too narrowly the lives of prelates and priests for fear I seem to have intended rather a satire than an oration, and be thought to tax good princes while I praise the bad. And therefore, what I slightly taught before has been to no other end but that it might appear that there's no man can live pleasantly unless he be initiated to my rites and have me propitious to him. For how can it be otherwise when Fortune, the great directress of all human affairs, and myself are so all one that she was always an enemy to those wise men, and on the contrary so favorable to fools and careless fellows that all things hit luckily to them?

You have heard of that Timotheus, the most fortunate general of the Athenians, of whom came that proverb, "His net caught fish, though he were asleep;" and that "The owl flies;" whereas these others hit properly, wise men "born in the fourth month;" and again, "He rides Sejanus's his horse;" and "gold of Toulouse," signifying thereby the extremity of ill fortune. But I forbear the further threading of proverbs, lest I seem to have pilfered my friend Erasmus' adages. Fortune loves those that have least wit and most confidence and such as like that saying of Caesar, "The die is thrown." But wisdom makes men bashful, which is the reason that those wise men have so little to do, unless it be with poverty, hunger, and chimney corners; that they live such neglected, unknown, and hated lives: whereas fools abound in money, have the chief commands in the commonwealth, and in a word, flourish every way. For if it be happiness to please princes and to be conversant among those golden and diamond gods, what is more unprofitable than wisdom, or what is it these kind of men have, may more justly be censured? If wealth is to be got, how little good at it is that merchant like to do, if following the precepts of wisdom, he should boggle at perjury; or being taken in a lie, blush; or in the least regard the sad scruples of those wise men touching rapine and usury. Again, if a man sue for honors or church preferments, an ass or wild ox shall sooner get them than a wise man. If a man's in love with a young wench, none of the least humors in this comedy, they are wholly addicted to fools and are afraid of a wise man

and fly him as they would a scorpion. Lastly, whoever intend to live merry and frolic, shut their doors
against wise men and admit anything sooner. In
brief, go whither you will, among prelates, princes,
judges, magistrates, friends, enemies, from highest
to lowest, and you'll find all things done by money;
which, as a wise man condemns it, so it takes a special care not to come near him. What shall I say?
There is no measure or end of my praises, and yet 'tis
fit my oration have an end. And therefore I'll even
break off; and yet, before I do it, 'twill not be amiss
if I briefly show you that there has not been wanting
even great authors that have made me famous, both
by their writings and actions, lest perhaps otherwise
I may seem to have foolishly pleased myself only, or
that the lawyers charge me that I have proved nothing. After their example, therefore, will I allege my
proofs, that is to say, nothing to the point.

And first, every man allows this proverb, "That
where a man wants matter, he may best frame some."
And to this purpose is that verse which we teach
children, " 'Tis the greatest wisdom to know when
and where to counterfeit the fool." And now judge
yourselves what an excellent thing this folly is, whose
very counterfeit and semblance only has got such
praise from the learned. But more candidly does that
fat plump "Epicurean bacon-hog," Horace, for so he

calls himself, bid us "mingle our purposes with folly;" and whereas he adds the word *bravem,* short, perhaps to help out the verse, he might as well have let it alone; and again, " 'Tis a pleasant thing to play the fool in the right season;" and in another place, he had rather "be accounted a dotterel and sot than to be wise and made mouths at." And Telemachus in Homer, whom the poet praises so much, is now and then called *nepios,* fool: and by the same name, as if there were some good fortune in it, are the tragedians wont to call boys and striplings. And what does that sacred book of Iliads contain but a kind of counter-scuffle between foolish kings and foolish people? Besides, how absolute is that praise that Cicero gives of it! "All things are full of fools." For who does not know that every good, the more diffusive it is, by so much the better it is?

But perhaps their authority may be of small credit among Christians. We'll therefore, if you please, support our praises with some testimonies of Holy Writ also, in the first place, nevertheless, having forespoke our theologians that they'll give us leave to do it without offense. And in the next, forasmuch as we attempt a matter of some difficulty and it may be perhaps a little too saucy to call back again the Muses from Helicon to so great a journey, especially in a matter they are wholly strangers to, it will be more suitable, perhaps, while I play the divine and make my way through such prickly quiddities, that I entreat the soul of Scotus, a thing more bristly than either porcupine or hedgehog, to leave his scorebone awhile and come into my breast, and then let him go whither he pleases, or to the dogs. I could wish also that I might change my countenance, or that I had on the square cap and the cassock, for fear some or other should impeach me of theft as if I had privily rifled our masters' desks in that I have got so much divinity. But it ought not to seem so strange if after so long and intimate an acquaintance and converse with them I have picked up somewhat; when as that fig-tree-god Priapus hearing his owner read certain Greek words took so much notice of them that he got them by heart, and that cock in Lucian by having lived long among men became at last a master of their language.

But to the point under a fortunate direction. Ecclesiastes says in his first chapter, "The number of fools is infinite;" and when he calls it infinite, does he not seem to comprehend all men, unless it be some few whom yet 'tis a question whether any man ever saw? But more ingeniously does Jeremiah in his tenth chapter confess it, saying, "Every man is made a fool through his own wisdom;" attributing wisdom to God alone and leaving folly to all men else,

and again, "Let not man glory in his wisdom." And
why, good Jeremiah, would you not have a man
glory in his wisdom? Because, he'll say, he has none
at all. But to return to Ecclesiastes, who, when he
cries out, "Vanity of vanities, all is vanity!" what
other thoughts had he, do you believe, than that, as
I said before, the life of man is nothing else but an
interlude of folly? In which he has added one voice
more to that justly received praise of Cicero's which
I quoted before, viz., "All things are full of fools."
Again, that wise preacher that said, "A fool changes
as the moon, but a wise man is permanent as the
sun," what else did he hint at in it but that all mankind are fools and the name of wise only proper to
God? For by the moon interpreters understand human nature, and by the sun, God, the only fountain
of light; with which agrees that which Christ himself in the Gospel denies, that anyone is to be called
good but one, and that is God. And then if he is a
fool that is not wise, and every good man according
to the Stoics is a wise man, it is no wonder if all mankind be concluded under folly. Again Solomon,
Chapter 15, "Foolishness," says he, "is joy to the
fool," thereby plainly confessing that without folly
there is no pleasure in life. To which is pertinent that
other, "He that increases knowledge, increases grief;
and in much understanding there is much indigna-

tion." And does he not plainly confess as much, Chapter 7, "The heart of the wise is where sadness is, but the heart of fools follows mirth"? by which you see, he thought it not enough to have learned wisdom without he had added the knowledge of me also. And if you will not believe me, take his own words, Chapter 1, "I gave my heart to know wisdom and knowledge, madness and folly." Where, by the way, 'tis worth your remark that he intended me somewhat extraordinary that he named me last. A preacher wrote it, and this you know is the order among churchmen, that he that is first in dignity comes last in place, as mindful, no doubt, whatever they do in other things, herein at least to observe the evangelical precept.

Besides, that folly is more excellent than wisdom the son of Sirach, whoever he was, clearly witnesses, Chapter 44, whose words, so help me, Hercules! I shall not once utter before you meet my induction with a suitable answer, according to the manner of those in Plato that dispute with Socrates. What things are more proper to be laid up with care, such as are rare and precious, or such as are common and of no account? Why do you give me no answer? Well, though you should dissemble, the Greek proverb will answer for you, "Foul water is thrown out of doors;" which, if any man shall be so ungracious as to condemn, let him know 'tis Aristotle's, the god of our masters. Is there any of you so very a fool as to leave jewels and gold in the street? In truth, I think not; in the most secret part of your house; nor is that enough; if there be any drawer in your iron chests more private than other, there you lay them; but dirt you throw out of doors. And therefore, if you so carefully lay up such things as you value and throw away what's vile and of no worth, is it not plain that wisdom, which he forbids a man to hide, is of less account than folly, which he commands him to cover? Take his own words, "Better is the man that hideth his folly than he that hideth his wisdom." Or what is that, when he attributes an upright mind without craft or malice to a fool, when a wise man the while thinks no man like himself? For so I understand that in his tenth chapter, "A fool walking by the way, being a fool himself, supposes all men to be fools like him." And is it not a sign of great integrity to esteem every man as good as himself, and when there is no one that leans not too much to other way, to be so frank yet as to divide his praises with another? Nor was this great king ashamed of the name when he says of himself that he is more foolish than any man. Nor did Paul, that great doctor of the Gentiles, writing to the Corinthians, unwillingly acknowledge it; "I speak," says he, "like a fool. I am more." As if it could be any dishonor to excel in folly.

But here I meet with a great noise of some that endeavor to peck out the crows' eyes; that is, to blind the doctors of our times and smoke out their eyes with new annotations; among whom my friend Erasmus, whom for honor's sake I often mention, deserves if not the first place yet certainly the second. O most foolish instance, they cry, and well becoming Folly herself! The apostle's meaning was wide enough from what you dream; for he spoke it not in this sense, that he would have them believe him a greater fool than the rest, but when he had said, "They are ministers of Christ, the same am I," and by way of boasting herein had equaled himself with to others, he added this by way of correction or checking himself, "I am more," as meaning that he was not only equal to the rest of the apostles in the work of the Gospel, but somewhat superior. And therefore, while he would have this received as a truth, lest nevertheless it might not relish their ears as being spoken with too much arrogance, he foreshortened his argument with the vizard of folly, "I speak like a fool," because he knew it was the prerogative of fools to speak what they like, and that too without offense. Whatever he thought when he wrote this, I leave it to them to discuss; for my own part, I follow those fat, fleshy, and vulgarly approved doctors, with whom, by Jupiter! a great part of the learned had rather err than follow them that understand the tongues, though they are never so much in the right. Not any of them make greater account of those smatterers at Greek than if they were daws. Especially when a no small professor, whose name I wittingly conceal lest those choughs should chatter at me that Greek proverb I have so often mentioned, "an ass at a harp," discoursing magisterially and theologically on this text, "I speak as a fool, I am more," drew a new thesis; and, which without the height of logic he could never have done, made this new subdivision—for I'll give you his own words, not only in form but matter also—"I speak like a fool," that is, if you look upon me as a fool for comparing myself with those false apostles, I shall seem yet a greater fool by esteeming myself before them; though the same person a little after, as forgetting himself, runs off to another matter.

But why do I thus staggeringly defend myself with one single instance? As if it were not the common privilege of divines to stretch heaven, that is Holy Writ, like a cheverel; and when there are many things in St. Paul that thwart themselves, which yet in their proper place do well enough if there be any credit to be given to St. Jerome that was

master of five tongues. Such was that of his at
Athens when having casually espied the inscription
of that altar, he wrested it into an argument to prove
the Christian faith, and leaving out all the other
words because they made against him, took notice
only of the two last, viz., "To the unknown God;"
and those too not without some alteration, for the
whole inscription was thus: "To the Gods of Asia,
Europe, and Africa; To the unknown and strange
Gods." And according to his example do the sons of
the prophets, who, forcing out here and there four
or five expressions and if need be corrupting the
sense, wrest it to their own purpose; though what
goes before and follows after make nothing to the
matter in hand, nay, be quite against it. Which yet
they do with so happy an impudence that oftentimes
the civilians envy them that faculty.

For what is it in a manner they may not hope for
success in, when this great doctor (I had almost
bolted out his name, but that I once again stand in
fear of the Greek proverb) has made a construction
on an expression of Luke, so agreeable to the mind of
Christ as are fire and water to one another. For when
the last point of danger was at hand, at which time
retainers and dependents are wont in a more special
manner to attend their protectors, to examine what
strength they have, and prepare for the encounter,

Christ, intending to take out of his disciples' minds all trust and confidence in such like defense, demands of them whether they wanted anything when he sent them forth so unprovided for a journey that they had neither shoes to defend their feet from the injuries of stones and briars nor the provision of a scrip to preserve them from hunger. And when they had denied that they wanted anything, he adds, "But now, he that hath a bag, let him take it, and likewise a scrip; and he that hath none, let him sell his coat and buy a sword." And now when the sum of all that Christ taught pressed only meekness, suffering, and contempt of life, who does not clearly perceive what he means in this place? to wit, that he might the more disarm his ministers, that neglecting not only shoes and scrip but throwing away their very coat, they might, being in a manner naked, the more readily and with less hindrance take in hand the work of the Gospel, and provide themselves of nothing but a sword, not such as thieves and murderers go up and down with, but the sword of the spirit that pierces the most inward parts, and so cuts off as it were at one blow all earthly affections, that they mind nothing but their duty to God. But see, I pray, whither this famous theologian wrests it. By the sword he interprets defense against persecution, and by the bag sufficient provision to carry it on. As if Christ having altered his mind, in that he sent out his disciples not so royally attended as he should have done, repented himself of his former instructions: or as forgetting that he had said, "Blessed are ye when ye are evil spoken of, despised, and persecuted, etc.," and forbade them to resist evil; for that the meek in spirit, not the proud, are blessed: or, lest remembering, I say, that he had compared them to sparrows and lilies, thereby minding them what small care they should take for the things of this life, was so far now from having them go forth without a sword that he commanded them to get one, though with the sale of their coat, and had rather they should go naked than want a brawling-iron by their sides. And to this, as under the word "sword" he conceives to be comprehended whatever appertains to the repelling of injuries, so under that of "scrip" he takes in whatever is necessary to the support of life. And so does this deep interpreter of the divine meaning bring forth the apostles to preach the doctrine of a crucified Christ, but furnished at all points with lances, slings, quarterstaffs, and bombards; lading them also with bag and baggage, lest perhaps it might not be lawful for them to leave their inn unless they were empty and fasting. Nor does he take the least notice of this, that he so willed the sword to be bought, reprehends it a little after and commands it to be sheathed; and that it was never heard that the apostles ever used or swords or bucklers against the Gentiles, though 'tis likely they had done it, if Christ had ever intended, as this doctor interprets.

There is another, too, whose name out of respect I pass by, a man of no small repute, who from those tents which Habakkuk mentions, "The tents of the land of Midian shall tremble," drew this exposition, that it was prophesied of the skin of Saint Bartholomew who was flayed alive. And why, forsooth, but because those tents were covered with skins? I was lately myself at a theological dispute, for I am often there, where when one was demanding what authority there was in Holy Writ that commands heretics to be convinced by fire rather than reclaimed by argument; a crabbed old fellow, and one whose supercilious gravity spoke him at least a doctor, answered in a great fume that Saint Paul had decreed it, who said, "Reject him that is a heretic, after once or twice admonition." And when he had sundry times, one after another, thundered out the same thing, and most men wondered what ailed the man, at last he explained it thus, making two words of one. "A heretic must be put to death." Some laughed, and yet there wanted not others to whom this exposition seemed plainly theological; which, when some, though those very few, opposed, they cut off the dis-

pute, as we say, with a hatchet, and the credit of so
uncontrollable an author. "Pray conceive me," said
he, "it is written, 'Thou shalt not suffer a witch to
live.' But every heretic bewitches the people; therefore, etc." And now, as many as were present admired the man's wit, and consequently submitted to
his decision of the question. Nor came it into any of
their heads that that law concerned only fortunetell-
ers, enchanters, and magicians, whom the Hebrews
call in their tongue "Mecaschephim," witches or
sorcerers: for otherwise, perhaps, by the same reason
it might as well have extended to fornication and
drunkenness.

But I foolishly run on in these matters, though
yet there are so many of them that neither Chrysip-
pus' nor Didymus' volumes are large enough to contain them. I would only desire you to consider this,
that if so great doctors may be allowed this liberty,
you may the more reasonably pardon even me also, a
raw, effeminate divine, if I quote not everything so
exactly as I should. And so at last I return to Paul.
"Ye willingly," says he, "suffer my foolishness,"
and again, "Take me as a fool," and further, "I
speak it not after the Lord, but as it were foolishly,"
and in another place, "We are fools for Christ's
sake." You have heard from how great an author
how great praises of folly; and to what other end,

but that without doubt he looked upon it as that one thing both necessary and profitable. "If anyone among ye," says he, "seem to be wise, let him be a fool that he may be wise." And in Luke, Jesus called those two disciples with whom he joined himself upon the way, "fools." Nor can I give you any reason why it should seem so strange when Saint Paul imputes a kind of folly even to God himself. "The foolishness of God," says he, "is wiser than men." Though yet I must confess that origin upon the place denies that this foolishness may be resembled to the uncertain judgment of men; of which kind is, that "the preaching of the cross is to them that perish foolishness."

But why am I so careful to no purpose that I thus run on to prove my matter by so many testimonies? when in those mystical Psalms Christ speaking to the Father says openly, "Thou knowest my foolishness." Nor is it without ground that fools are so acceptable to God. The reason perhaps may be this, that as princes carry a suspicious eye upon those that are over-wise, and consequently hate them—as Caesar did Brutus and Cassius, when he feared not in the least drunken Antony; so Nero, Seneca; and Dionysius, Plato—and on the contrary are delighted in those blunter and unlabored wits, in like manner Christ ever abhors and condemns those wise men and such as put confidence in their own wisdom. And this Paul makes clearly out when he said, "God hath chosen the foolish things of this world," as well knowing it had been impossible to have reformed it by wisdom. Which also he sufficiently declares himself, crying out by the mouth of his prophet, "I will destroy the wisdom of the wise, and cast away the understanding of the prudent."

And again, when Christ gives Him thanks that He had concealed the mystery of salvation from the wise, but revealed it to babes and sucklings, that is to say, fools. For the Greek word for babes is fools, which he opposes to the word wise men. To this appertains that throughout the Gospel you find him ever accusing the Scribes and Pharisees and doctors of the law, but diligently defending the ignorant multitude (for what other is that "Woe to ye Scribes and Pharisees" than woe to you, you wise men?), but seems chiefly delighted in little children, women, and fishers. Besides, among brute beasts he is best pleased with those that have least in them of the foxes' subtlety. And therefore he chose rather to ride upon an ass when, if he had pleased, he might have bestrode the lion without danger. And the Holy Ghost came down in the shape of a dove, not of an eagle or kite. Add to this that in Scripture there is frequent mention of harts, hinds, and lambs; and

such as are destined to eternal life are called sheep,
than which creature there is not anything more foolish, if we may believe that proverb of Aristotle
"sheepish manners," which he tells us is taken from
the foolishness of that creature and is used to be
applied to dull-headed people and lack-wits. And yet
Christ professes to be the shepherd of this flock and
is himself delighted with the name of a lamb; according to Saint John, "Behold the Lamb of God!"
Of which also there is much mention in the Revela-
tion. And what does all this drive at, but that all
mankind are fools—nay, even the very best?

And Christ himself, that he might the better re-
lieve this folly, being the wisdom of the Father, yet
in some manner became a fool when taking upon
him the nature of man, he was found in shape as a
man; as in like manner he was made sin that he
might heal sinners. Nor did he work this cure any
other way than by the foolishness of the cross and a
company of fat apostles, not much better, to whom
also he carefully recommended folly but gave them a
caution against wisdom and drew them together by
the example of little children, lilies, mustard-seed,
and sparrows, things senseless and inconsiderable,
living only by the dictates of nature and without
either craft or care. Besides, when he forbade them to
be troubled about what they should say before gov-

ernors and straightly charged them not to inquire
after times and seasons, to wit, that they might not
trust to their own wisdom but wholly depend on
him. And to the same purpose is it that that great
Architect of the World, God, gave man an injunction
against his eating of the Tree of Knowledge, as if
knowledge were the bane of happiness; according to
which also, St. Paul disallows it as puffing up and
destructive; whence also St. Bernard seems in my
opinion to follow when he interprets that mountain
whereon Lucifer had fixed his habitation to be the
mountain of knowledge.

Nor perhaps ought I to omit this other argument,
that Folly is so gracious above that her errors are only
pardoned, those of wise men never. Whence it is
that they that ask forgiveness, though they offend
never so wittingly, cloak it yet with the excuse of
folly. So Aaron, in Numbers, if I mistake not the
book, when he sues unto Moses concerning his sister's leprosy, "I beseech thee, my Lord, not to lay
this sin upon us, which we have foolishly committed." So Saul makes his excuse of David, "For behold," says he, "I did it foolishly." And again,
David himself thus sweetens God, "And therefore I
beseech thee, O Lord, to take away the trespass of
thy servant, for I have done foolishly," as if he knew
there was no pardon to be obtained unless he had

colored his offense with folly and ignorance. And stronger is that of Christ upon the cross when he prayed for his enemies, "Father, forgive them," nor does he cover their crime with any other excuse than that of unwittingness—because, says he, "they know not what they do." In like manner Paul, writing to Timothy, "But therefore I obtained mercy, for that I did it ignorantly through unbelief." And what is the meaning of "I did it ignorantly" but that I did it out of folly, not malice? And what of "Therefore I received mercy" but that I had not obtained it had I not been made more allowable through the covert of folly? For us also makes that mystical Psalmist, though I remembered it not in its right place, "Remember not the sins of my youth nor my ignorances." You see what two things he pretends, to wit, youth, whose companion I ever am, and ignorances, and that in the plural number, a number of multitude, whereby we are to understand that there was no small company of them.

But not to run too far in that which is infinite. To speak briefly, all Christian religion seems to have a kind of alliance with folly and in no respect to have any accord with wisdom. Of which if you expect proofs, consider first that boys, old men, women, and fools are more delighted with religious and sacred things than others, and to that purpose are ever next the altars; and this they do by mere impulse of nature. And in the next place, you see that those first founders of it were plain, simple persons and most bitter enemies of learning. Lastly there are no sort of fools seem more out of the way than are these whom the zeal of Christian religion has once swallowed up; so that they waste their estates, neglect injuries, suffer themselves to be cheated, put no difference between friends and enemies, abhor pleasure, are crammed with poverty, watchings, tears, labors, reproaches, loathe life, and wish death above all things; in short, they seem senseless to common understanding, as if their minds lived elsewhere and not in their own bodies; which, what else is it than to be mad? For which reason you must not think it so strange if the apostles seemed to be drunk with new wine, and if Paul appeared to Festus to be mad.

But now, having once gotten on the lion's skin, go to, and I'll show you that this happiness of Christians, which they pursue with so much toil, is nothing else but a kind of madness and folly; far be it that my words should give any offense, rather consider my matter. And first, the Christians and Platonists do as good as agree in this, that the soul is plunged and fettered in the prison of the body, by the grossness of which it is so tied up and hindered that it cannot take a view of or enjoy things as they truly are; and for that cause their master defines philosophy to be a contemplation of death, because it takes off the mind from visible and corporeal objects, than which death does no more. And therefore, as long as the soul uses the organs of the body in that right manner it ought, so long it is said to be in good state and condition; but when, having broken its fetters, it endeavors to get loose and assays, as it were, a flight out of that prison that holds it in, they call it madness; and if this happen through any distemper or indisposition of the organs, then, by the common consent of every man, 'tis downright madness. And yet we see such kind of men foretell things to come, understand tongues and letters they never learned before, and seem, as it were, big with a kind of divinity. Nor is it to be doubted but that it proceeds from hence, that the mind, being somewhat at liberty from the infection of the body, begins to put forth itself in its native vigor. And I conceive 'tis from the same cause that the like often happens to sick men a little before their death, that they discourse in strain above mortality as if they were inspired. Again, if this happens upon the score of religion, though perhaps it may not be the same kind of madness, yet 'tis so near it that a great many men would judge it no better, especially when a few inconsiderable people shall differ from the rest of the world in the whole course of their life. And therefore it fares with them as, according to the fiction of Plato, happens to those that being cooped up in a cave stand gaping with admiration at the shadows of things; and that fugitive who, having broke from them and returning to them again, told them he had seen things truly as they were, and that they were the most mistaken in believing there was nothing but pitiful shadows. For as this wise man pitied and bewailed their palpable madness that were possessed with so gross an error, so they in return laughed at him as a doting fool and cast him out of their company. In like manner the common sort of men chiefly admire those things that are most corporeal and almost believe there is nothing beyond them. Whereas on the contrary, these devout persons, by how much the nearer anything concerns the body, by so much more they neglect it and are wholly hurried away with the contemplation of things invisible. For the one give the first place to riches, the next to their corporeal pleasures, leaving the last place to their soul, which yet most of them do scarce believe, because they can't see it with their eyes. On the contrary, the others first rely wholly on God, the most unchangeable of all things; and next him, yet on this that comes nearest him, they bestow the second on their soul; and lastly, for their body, they neglect that care and condemn and fly money as superfluity that may be well spared; or if they are forced to meddle with any of these things, they do it carelessly and much against their wills, having as if they had it not, and possessing as if they possessed it not.

There are also in each several things several degrees wherein they disagree among themselves. And first as to the senses, though all of them have more or less affinity with the body, yet of these some are more gross and blockish, as tasting, hearing, seeing, smelling, touching; some more removed from the body, as memory, intellect, and the will. And therefore to which of these the mind applies itself, in that lies its force. But holy men, because the whole bent of their minds is taken up with those things that are most repugnant to these grosser senses, they seem brutish and stupid in the common use of them. Whereas on the contrary, the ordinary sort of people are best at these, and can do least at the other; from whence it is, as we have heard, that some of these holy men have by mistake drunk oil for wine. Again, in the affections of the mind, some have a greater commerce with the body than others, as lust, desire of meat and sleep, anger, pride, envy; with which holy men are at irreconcilable enmity, and contrary, the common people think there's no living without

them. And lastly there are certain middle kind of
affections, and as it were natural to every man, as the
love of one's country, children, parents, friends, and
to which the common people attribute no small matter; whereas the other strive to pluck them out of
their mind: unless insomuch as they arrive to that
highest part of the soul, that they love their parents
not as parents—for what did they get but the body?
though yet we owe it to God, not them—but as good
men or women and in whom shines the image of
that highest wisdom which alone they call the chiefest good, and out of which, they say, there is nothing to be beloved or desired.

And by the same rule do they measure all things
else, so that they make less account of whatever is
visible, unless it be altogether contemptible, than of
those things which they cannot see. But they say
that in Sacraments and other religious duties there is
both body and spirit. As in fasting they count it not
enough for a man to abstain from eating, which the
common people take for an absolute fast, unless there
be also a lessening of his depraved affections: as that
he be less angry, less proud, than he was wont, that
the spirit, being less clogged with its bodily weight,
may be the more intent upon heavenly things. In
like manner, in the Eucharist, though, say they, it
is not to be esteemed the less that 'tis administered

with ceremonies, yet of itself 'tis of little effect, if not hurtful, unless that which is spiritual be added to it, to wit, that which is represented under those visible signs. Now the death of Christ is represented by it, which all men, vanquishing, abolishing, and, as it were, burying their carnal affections, ought to express in their lives and conversations that they may grow up to a newness of life and be one with him and the same one among another. This a holy man does, and in this is his only meditation. Whereas on the contrary, the common people think there's no more in that sacrifice than to be present at the altar and crowd next it, to have a noise of words and look upon the ceremonies. Nor in this alone, which we only proposed by way of example, but in all his life, and without hypocrisy, does a holy man fly those things that have any alliance with the body and is wholly ravished with things eternal, invisible, and spiritual. For which cause there's so great contrariety of opinion between them, and that too in everything, that each party thinks the other out of their wits; though that character, in my judgment, better agrees with those holy men than the common people: which yet will be more clear if, as I promised, I briefly show you that that great reward they so much fancy is nothing else but a kind of madness.

And therefore suppose that Plato dreamed of

somewhat like it when he called the madness of lovers the most happy condition of all others. For he that's violently in love lives not in his own body but in the thing he loves; and by how much the farther he runs from himself into another, by so much the greater is his pleasure. And then, when the mind strives to rove from its body and does not rightly use its own organs, without doubt you may say 'tis downright madness and not be mistaken, or otherwise what's the meaning of those common sayings, "He does not dwell at home," "Come to yourself," "He's his own man again"? Besides, the more perfect and true his love is, the more pleasant is his madness. And therefore, what is that life hereafter, after which these holy minds so pantingly breathe, like to be? To wit, the spirit shall swallow up the body, as conqueror and more durable; and this it shall do with the greater ease because heretofore, in its lifetime, it had cleansed and thinned it into such another nothing as itself. And then the spirit again shall be wonderfully swallowed up by the highest mind, as being more powerful than infinite parts; so that the whole man is to be out of himself nor to be otherwise happy in any respect, but that being stripped of himself, he shall participate of somewhat ineffable from that chiefest good that draws all things into itself. And this happiness though 'tis only then perfected when souls being joined to their former bodies shall be made immortal, yet forasmuch as the life of holy men is nothing but a continued meditation and, as it were, shadow of that life, it so happens that at length they have some taste or relish of it; which, though it be but as the smallest drop in comparison of that fountain of eternal happiness, yet it far surpasses all worldly delight, though all the pleasures of all mankind were all joined together. So much better are things spiritual than things corporeal, and things invisible than things visible; which doubtless is that which the prophet promises: "The eye hath not seen, nor the ear heard, nor has it entered into the heart of man to consider what God has provided for them that love Him." And this is that Mary's better part which is not taken away by change of life, but perfected.

And therefore they that are sensible of it, and few there are to whom this happens, suffer a kind of somewhat little differing from madness; for they utter many things that do not hang together, and that too not after the manner of men but make a kind of sound which they neither heed themselves, nor is it understood by others, and change the whole figure of their countenance, one while jocund, another while dejected, now weeping, then laughing, and again sighing. And when they come to themselves, tell you they know not where they have been, whether in the body or out of the body, or sleeping; nor do they remember what they have heard, seen, spoken, or done, and only know this, as it were in a mist or dream, that they were the most happy while they were so out of their wits. And therefore they are sorry they are come to themselves again and desire nothing more than this kind of madness, to be perpetually mad. And this is a small taste of that future happiness.

But I forget myself and run beyond my bounds. Though yet, if I shall seem to have spoken anything more boldly or impertinently than I ought, be pleased to consider that not only Folly but a woman said it; remembering in the meantime that Greek proverb, "Sometimes a fool may speak a word in season," unless perhaps you expect an epilogue, but give me leave to tell you you are mistaken if you think I remember anything of what I have said, having foolishly bolted out such a hodgepodge of words. 'Tis an old proverb, "I hate one that remembers what's done over the cup." This is a new one of my own making: I hate a man that remembers what he hears. Wherefore farewell, clap your hands, live and drink lustily, my most excellent disciples of Folly.

Finis

ANN ARBOR PAPERBACKS

reissues of works of enduring merit

The University of Michigan Press / Ann Arbor